NO OTHER GODS

NO OTHER GODS

PURSUING YOUR PASSION FOR JESUS AND BASKETBALL

SEASON 1

RELIGION / Christian Living / Devotional

By
By Kari Kieper

XULON PRESS ELITE

Xulon Press
2301 Lucien Way #415
Maitland, FL 32751
407.339.4217
www.xulonpress.com

Unless otherwise indicated, Scripture quotations taken from the Holy Bible, New International Version (NIV). Copyright © 1973, 1978, 1984, 2011 by Biblica, Inc.™. Used by permission. All rights reserved.

Scripture quotations taken from the King James Version (KJV) – *public domain.*

Scripture quotations taken from the New American Standard Bible (NASB). Copyright © 1960, 1962, 1963, 1968, 1971, 1972, 1973, 1975, 1977, 1995 by The Lockman Foundation. Used by permission. All rights reserved.

Printed in the United States of America.

ISBN-13: 978-1-6312-9129-6

TO CAEDEN AND CAILYN MARIE,

WATCHING YOU PLAY BASKETBALL THROUGHOUT the years has been a treasured gift. I have hurt with you. I have rejoiced with you. I have experienced defeat with you. I have experienced victory with you. I have cried with you. I have laughed with you. Of all those experiences, the best part has been *with you!* Thank you for the memories!

ACKNOWLEDGMENTS

MY HEART OVERFLOWS WITH THANKSGIVING for my extraordinary friend and accountability partner, Meredith McSpadden. You have journeyed with me every step of the way as I wrote this book. I will always cherish our monthly accountability meetings in a French bakery at "our table" where you faithfully tracked my progress and gracefully spurred me on to complete the good work that God had started. Thank you, Meredith, for pouring into my life even in the midst of personal loss in your own. For that, I am eternally grateful.

To a special group of student-athletes who were intentionally chosen to critique portions of *No Other Gods,* thank you! I cannot fully express my appreciation for the time you carved out of your busy schedules to provide your feedback. Your reactions, comments, and suggestions were extremely valuable. So thank you Zion, EJ, Natalie, Caeden, and Cailyn for your input! May the Lord continue to bless your basketball journeys and academic ambitions.

To Robin Winkles, thank you for contributing your time and talents to this project. You are gifted in so many ways, and I am honored that you would choose to use your editing and photography skills in the creation of this book.

To every individual who has prayed for me along the way, thank you from the bottom of my heart! From my immediate family and cherished friends, to my church family, pastors, and countless others who have interceded on my behalf, I hope you feel, in some part, responsible for the very book you hold in your hands. Your prayers have been a source of encouragement for me.

To my friends at Casa Costa Bake Shop, thank you for allowing me to sit in your cozy eatery for hours on end working on this book; a place where hot coffee and fresh ideas were always brewing!

To my devoted husband, Kevin, thank you for your unending support and for believing in me. Your faith in my vision made it possible for me to keep pressing forward. Thank you for continually expressing how proud you are of me and for loving me so beautifully. You are loved and appreciated more than you know and more than I'm capable of showing.

And finally, I am so thankful to Jesus for allowing me to see his reflection in a 28.5-inch ball and for allowing me opportunities to minister through the game of basketball, not only to youth but to an assortment of ages. It's been a source of overwhelming joy!

INTRODUCTION

IT WAS APRIL, 2017. BEFORE LONG OUR FAMILY would be headed in different directions to watch our kids play in summer basketball tournaments across the state of Texas and beyond. My role at church would be put on hold and worship services would be replaced with basketball tournaments. Our family recognized the commitment to summer basketball would affect our attendance at church, but we also recognized it didn't have to alter our commitment to worship God. Kevin and I would be intentional about not allowing summer basketball to become an idol of sorts; we would not forsake Christ in the midst of pursuing basketball ambitions.

And so it was. In an effort to keep Christ first, we attended worship services in whatever city or state we were in if the tournament schedule allowed. If it wasn't possible, then we made it a point to sit down with our kids on Sunday night or a weeknight to watch an online sermon together. Afterwards, we would have a time of reflection and talk about how we might apply the message in our own lives. That's how our family created worship experiences during the height of summer basketball. But we are just one family. What about the countless number of other families who might not know how to create their own worship experience?

That question burned in my brain. How can the Word of God easily be put into athletes' hands while they're at tournaments? Why do they have to miss out on worship experiences because they're chasing after scholarships to support a higher education? And then...God planted a seed in my heart—create worship experiences in the form of basketball devotionals to inspire and motivate players, parents, coaches, and fans by using basketball analogies to teach His Word. I began to have a vision of athletes packing their backpacks with their uniform, court shoes, ball, and their "basketball bible." I had a vision of parents and players setting aside fifteen minutes to read a lesson together in their hotel room prior to Sunday games. I had a vision of teams circling in hotel lobbies and taking time to focus on God's Word before heading to the gym. I had a vision of a spiritually committed player crouched in the corner of a gym reading a lesson between games as an act of worship. I had more and more visions. And then I began to write biblical lessons basketball players could relate to.

The lessons in this book are challenging. Even now, the Lord is continuing to refine me by making me walk through the very lessons I am teaching you about. There are days when I fail miserably. I get frustrated with the coach. I yell at the refs. I get stuck on stats. I allow pressure to rattle me. I take my eyes off God's perspective. I become weary. I grumble instead of pray. But in all that, God's grace is greater than all my sin and His mercies are new every day! The truth of God's Word, weaved throughout these pages, speaks to me over and over again. With the empowering work of the Holy Spirit, I will continue to move further away from fleshly responses and move closer to the character of Christ. That is also my hope for you!

I encourage you to use this devotional book in whatever ways you think will honor the Lord and strengthen your walk with Him. Whether it's for personal growth, a weekend devotional, a monthly bible study, a source for team devotionals, or to learn about your Heavenly Father for the first time, I hope your fellowship with Him becomes sweeter and sweeter as you gain a greater knowledge of His love for you. Not only that, but I hope you will be inspired to practice and play like there's no tomorrow.

"So leave everything on the court.
Leave the game better than you found it.
And when it comes time for you to leave, leave a legend."
Kobe Bryant
August 23, 1978 – January 26, 2020

TABLE OF CONTENTS

PREGAME

Dedication v

Acknowledgments vii

Introduction ix

TIP OFF

1. No Other Gods, Part One 1

2. No Other Gods, Part Two 9

TIME OUT: THE FUNDAMENTALS

3. Fundamental #1: Don't Believe the Lies 17

4. Fundamental #2: Let's Talk About Sin 24

5. Fundamental #3: What Exactly Is a Christian? 30

6. Fundamental #4: Joining Team Jesus. 37

7. Fundamental #5: I've Made a Formal Commitment.

   Now What?. 41

BACK IN THE GAME

8. A Matter of Perspective 51

9. Infallible Help Defense 57

10. Heavy Lifting Is Light Work 65

11. How's Your Availability? 71

12. Respecting Authority—It Really Is Black and White 77

13. Composure vs. Pressure 85

14. Denying Your Man 93

15. No Holding Back. 101

16. The Consolation Prize 107

17. Work While You Wait. 113

POSTGAME

Epilogue 119

False Gods

Idolatry consists, not only in the worship of false gods,
but also in the worship of the True God in false ways.
Alistair Begg

The more time and devotion one spends
in the worship of false gods,
the less he is able to spend in that of the True One.
Isaac Newton

If you uproot the idol and fail to plant the love of Christ
in its place, the idol will grow back.
Tullvan Tchividjian

CHAPTER 1
NO OTHER GODS,
Part One

You shall have no other gods before me.
Exodus 20:3 (NIV)

"BALL IS LIFE." YOU'VE HEARD THE EXPRESSION and you've seen the t-shirts. Perhaps you've even worn one. "Ball is Life" also refers to a group of professional producers who express their love of basketball through mixtapes, apparel, and social media highlights designed to enthuse basketball lovers across the world.[1] Sure, I understand it's just a saying, but that short, powerful phrase has always left me feeling somewhat unsettled. Perhaps I'm taking the expression *way* too seriously, but my reverential fear of the Lord screams, *"Jesus is Life!"*

I began wondering about the origin of "ball is life," so I decided to do some research. The result? My personal conviction was affirmed through Dictionary.com: "Ball is life refers to the all-consuming passion basketball players and fans have for the game. Ball is life doesn't just signify being a fan of the game; it represents someone who loves and lives for the game, plays as much as they can, thinks about it when they can't play, and finds meaning in their lives through basketball."[2]

Yikes! That sounds dangerously like idolatry to me. Sound far-fetched? Let me assure you, idolatry is alive and well and is trying to work its way into our hearts to distract us from worshipping the

One True God. In the words of the French theologian, John Calvin, "The human heart is an idol factory."

So what is an idol, why are idols dangerous, and what does idolatry look like in today's world? Pastor John Piper puts it this way: "Idolatry starts in the heart: craving, wanting, enjoying, being satisfied by anything that you treasure more than God. It is the thing loved or the person loved more than God, desired more than God, treasured more than God, and enjoyed more than God."[3] And yes, this can include *good* things such as basketball, relationships and careers.

I have no idea where you are in your Christian walk, so maybe this idea of idolatry is foreign to you, but you should know God takes idols very seriously. So how do we figure out what our individual idols are? This is challenging because sometimes idolatry can creep up on us and it can be hard to recognize. Therefore, the objective of this lesson is to take a close look at your life and determine if you have unknowingly set up any false idols in your heart.

As we consider the truth of God's Word and what He has to say about idolatry, ask the Holy Spirit to convict your heart and show you any areas in your life where you could be misplacing your passion for something or someone in place of Him. As you closely examine your heart, it is *incredibly* important you don't confuse *conviction* for *condemnation*. Conviction comes from the Holy Spirit and it's a good thing. The Holy Spirit convicts us when we are heading in the wrong direction and when we are in sin. When you are convicted, you may feel disappointed in yourself or heavy-hearted. When the Holy Spirit is convicting you, pay attention! The Spirit of the Lord is leading you to repentance and to turn towards God so that your sins may be wiped out and times of refreshing may come (Acts 3:19).

On the other hand, condemnation is a tool of Satan and it's a bad thing. He wants you to feel the weight of guilt and shame. He wants you to play mistakes over and over again in your mind, telling you you're no good—that you're a failure. But that's a lie! DO NOT fall for it! The key to living victoriously is to keep your eyes on Christ and who *He* says you are! So, from this day forward, I hope you never forget the difference between conviction and condemnation. Guilt, shame, regret, and depression can land you in a spiritual prison, but God's finished work on the cross has already set you free! There is no condemnation for those who are in Christ Jesus (Rom. 8:1).

Now that that's settled, let's dig into scripture beginning with Exodus 20:3-4. Here, we find the first two commandments God gave Moses on Mount Sinai: "You shall have no other gods before me," and "You shall not make for yourself an image in the form of anything in heaven above or on the earth beneath or in the waters below." And why is that? Exodus 34:14 gives us just *one* of the reasons: "Do not worship any other god, for the LORD, whose name is Jealous, is a jealous God." Let's be clear, God is not jealous *of you*, He is jealous *for you*. He wants your time and attention before any of your other passions. He created you to be in fellowship with Him, so when we chase after hobbies, sports, careers, people, and "things" over God, it can be dangerous because idolatry is a sin and sin separates us from God. "But your iniquities have separated you from your God; your sins have hidden his face from you, so that he will not hear" (Isa. 59:2).

So how can basketball become an idol? Let's go back to our definition of "ball is life." If basketball has become your all-consuming passion, it's an idol. If you love and live for the game, it has become your idol. If you play as much as you can and think about it when you're not playing, it's prob-ably an idol. If you find meaning for your life through the game of basket-ball, it's likely an idol. *Jesus* wants to be your all-consuming passion. *Jesus* wants you to love and live for *Him*. *Jesus* wants you to find meaning for your life through *Him*. This doesn't

This doesn't mean you push aside basketball for Jesus, but don't push aside Jesus for basketball.

3

mean you push aside basketball for Jesus, but don't push aside Jesus for basketball. After all, He's the one who put a passion in your heart to play the game.

Recall the last seven days. How much time did you spend each day with a ball in your hands? How much time did you spend at practice? With your trainer? At tournaments or games? On the other hand, how much time did you spend reading your Bible or devotional book? How much time did you spend in prayer each day? How much time did you spend thinking about spiritual things? The time you spend focused on spiritual growth *does not* have to balance with the time you spend practicing and elevating your game, but when basketball becomes an all-consuming passion, there's a definite breach of the first two commandments.

For today, let's chew on what we've talked about so far. In our next lesson we will attempt to uncover some other areas where we might be tempted to build false gods within the framework of our lives. If you're already beginning to feel a stirring in your belly, take a moment to thank the Lord for the work of the Holy Spirit as He begins to transform your thinking.

CHALK TALK

Player Application

I met a delightful young woman recently who is bringing the light of Christ to college athletes on the University of Texas campus. She began kicking a soccer ball around the age of four, started playing competitively in third grade, and went on to play in college. Soccer was her life and it's where she found her worth. However, after tearing her ACL three times, the doctor told her to hang up her cleats for good. For the next two years, she searched for purpose in very dark places. During her senior year of college, she finally began to allow Jesus into her life and He completely transformed her! God has now called her to bring His light and love into the darkness that hides in college athletics.

When your worth and identity are wrapped up in being an athlete, you may be making an idol out of your sport. What if basketball was taken away from you? Would you be enough without it? Christ wants our identity to be in Him and Him alone. For *only* He is worthy of our worship!

Coach Application

It's easy to spend hours upon hours breaking down game film, reviewing stats, making practice plans, learning new offensive sets, and preparing for your next match up. I know what it's like to let your team's success and win-loss record rule your mind, but when it overtakes you, that's when coaching can become something of an idol. Does your life center around coaching or do you allow Jesus to be the center of your coaching? Staying firmly planted in God's word on a consistent basis will allow you to keep God first and coaching in its rightful place.

Parent Application

When my two teenagers picked up basketball at a very young age, I knew club basketball could eventually prevent us from attending Sunday worship. I noticed young families vanishing from the church pews during the spring and summer months. I knew some were playing in tournaments and I also knew, as much as I didn't want to believe it, this could likely be us someday. Sure enough, that "someday" is now. We find ourselves out of town most summer weekends, often split in different directions. Despite our hectic schedules, we have a blast watching our kids compete! However, between tournaments, practices, trainings, and games, it's easy for us to make our kids and basketball the center of our lives. But amid the chaos, it is our responsibility to make sure we don't lose sight of seeking the Lord in all that we do. One way our family does this is by making an attempt to attend a local worship service between tournament games, even if it means showing up in our team apparel. If game schedules and worship times conflict, we try to assemble together another night of the week to watch a sermon online. Afterwards, we talk about how we can apply the message in our lives. It's a statement to our kids about how we love and live for Jesus first and foremost.

PERSONAL TRAINING SESSION

- After reading today's lesson, do you have reason to believe you might have some "false gods" in your life? If so, list them below. In the next lesson, we will see if any items from your list appear.

_____

_____

- Conviction can make us feel very uncomfortable, but why is it a good thing?

_____

_____

- Condemnation is a tool Satan uses to mess with our heads. It's one of his most powerful tools and can do massive damage. Be careful! We use that same tool. Read Romans 2:1. Why is it wrong to judge others?

_____

_____

POST-GAME PRAYER

Heavenly Father, I humbly approach Your throne of grace, acknowledging there is but one God, the Father, from whom all things come and for whom we live; and there is but one Lord, Jesus Christ! (1 Cor. 8:6). Open my eyes so I may slowly begin to recognize areas in my life that have taken my time, attention, and passion away from You. I accept that I have unintentionally constructed false idols in my life by "worshipping" those things that can only bring temporary happiness. I give the Holy Spirit full authority to convict my heart when I am putting my passions for basketball or other things above my passion for You. Remind me that condemnation is a tool of Satan and he not only wants me to feel the weight of it, but also to participate in it. I stand against that trickery and I stand with You! Amen.

Idolatry

Our affections will never rise to things above if we give
them endless satisfaction to things below.
John Piper

Idolatry happens when we take good things
and make them ultimate things.
Timothy Keller

Nothing teaches us about the preciousness of the Creator
as much as when we learn the emptiness of everything else.
Charles Spurgeon

CHAPTER 2
NO OTHER GODS,
PART TWO

Seek first the kingdom of God and his righteousness
and all these things will be added to you.
Matthew 6:33 (ESV)

IN PART ONE OF "NO OTHER GODS," WE CONSID-
ered the idea that basketball can become an idol if God is not
held in His rightful place. So where is God's rightful place? God's
rightful place is *every* place! God is omnipresent. That's a long
word for "present everywhere at the same time." Thus, God is
with you every second of the day no matter where you are, but
He wants *you* to be in collaboration with Him. You have a choice.
You can go through life walking hand-in-hand with the Lord or you
can rely on yourself.

Look at it this way—have you ever had a teammate who
played "me ball?" If you have, then you would agree it's very frustrating! Let me set the scene: you are wide open; feet are set and
balanced. Your hands are up, ready to catch and shoot, but your
teammate keeps the ball, dribbles down the middle of the lane,
right into three defenders and forces a shot that gets rejected
out of bounds! Really? Yet, there you were, in perfect position
to score. What was the problem? The problem was a teammate
who gave into his own selfish desires, for his own satisfaction and
his own selfish gain, oblivious to you. I believe many of us are like

that "me ball" player. We reject God by selfishly doing what *we* want to do to fill a craving or gain attention, oblivious to the fact that He is right there waiting to help us succeed. Sadly, many of us are looking to false gods to fill a certain satisfaction, craving or to meet our needs, which really aren't *needs* at all.

Satan couldn't be more pleased that idolatry continues to keep God at arm's length in the lives of many Christians today. In our last lesson, I told you we would attempt to uncover some areas in our lives where we may have created some false gods. Take a look at the list below. How many of these passions do you crave more than God, treasure more than God, or enjoy more than God? This is a good time to remind you about the difference between conviction and condemnation, from part one. Condemnation is from the devil and it's a bad thing. Conviction is from the Holy Spirit and it's a good thing.

- *Cell phone.* Are you as dependent on Christ as you are your phone? Can you imagine not checking your social media apps for a single day, yet you go days without checking in with Jesus?
- *Netflix.* Do you spend hours upon hours binge watching your favorite shows but you can't set aside five or ten minutes a day with the Lord?
- *SnapChat.* A "streak" indicates direct snaps back and forth with a friend for several consecutive days. Snapchat even rewards long streaks with special emojis! Do you have a streak with Jesus? He rewards your faithfulness even more so!
- *Instagram.* Are you fixated on who's following you and how many "likes" your photo got? Jesus wants you to follow *Him*. Forget the filters! He approves of you just the way you are!

- *YouTube.* How many hours do you log watching your favorite YouTuber, pop star, gamer, rapper or athlete? Do their latest vlogs bring value to your life the way God's Word can?
- *Sneakers & Hypebeast Culture.* How much time do you spend passionately studying sneakers? Are you obsessed with trying to purchase the latest release? Is your mind consumed with collecting fashion pieces that are "hype" in order to impress others or make yourself feel good? Are you infatuated with wearing the most exclusive clothing labels, that cost a high price, but you neglect Jesus's gift of salvation, which also cost a high price?
- *Girlfriend/boyfriend.* If you're worshipping the ground they walk on, you're worshipping the wrong person. And if your guy or gal isn't interested in a relationship with Jesus Christ, save yourself some heartache and break it off now (that's another lesson for another time).
- *Video games.* Do you spend extended periods of time trying to master the game? Beware! The game could end up mastering you. Matthew 6:24 says no one can serve two masters.
- *Grades/Career.* Yes, even grades or a job can become an obsession. God wants your identity and worth to be found in Him, not in your grades or job performance. Yes, He wants excellence from you, but He wants your heart first.
- *Money.* Are you guilty of putting too much emphasis on money, to the point of even posting pictures of it? "For the love of money is the root of all kinds of evil. Some people, eager for money, have wandered from the true faith and pierced themselves with many griefs" (1 Tim. 6:10 AMP).
- *Drugs, alcohol, sexual impurity.* If you're looking for any of these things to save you from anxiety, depression, or loneliness, then you're looking in the wrong direction. They will

only dig a deeper pit. *Nothing* but Jesus can fill that God-shaped hole in your heart.

I could go on and on but I think you get the picture. Make no mistake! I love my phone. I love Lifetime Movie Network (yes, I said it). I love NetFlix. I love to watch talent and singing shows. I love fashion. I love basketball. But I *really love* God. And no, I don't always show it. I don't always reflect it. And I don't always live it. But I want to! That's why *No Other Gods* is so important. It's not just a message for you, but a reminder to me, and a warning for us all to be mindful, *every day,* of where and with whom our loyalty lies.

So how do we keep from allowing any of these "good things" to become our little "g" gods? The answer is found in Matthew 6:33 where we are told to seek first the kingdom of God and His righteousness. *Seek. God. First.* Do you want to show God that He is your number one? Then *seek* (search for, look for, hunt for, be in quest of) *God first.* As you do this, He will begin to fuel your passion for Him and give you a fulfillment that no sport, sneaker, girl, guy, video game, money, or social media app could ever give you!

I used to be a night owl. Staying up late was enjoyable. I got so much accomplished in the quiet of the night while the rest of my family was tucked in bed. In 2012, I was invited to take a discipleship class called "One on One with God." It gave me the tools necessary to develop a relationship with Christ that was richer and more gratifying than I ever dreamed possible. It was during this intense, fifteen-week period that I *learned* to get up early and seek God first thing in the morning. It was hard. It was really hard. Did I mention how hard it was? It took me a long time to get in the habit of going to bed earlier and waking up earlier. The process is not going to happen overnight for you. It's not even going to happen in a month or year. It's a *lifelong process* of seeking Christ e-v-e-r-y-d-a-y. You will have days when it's not possible to read your Bible for one reason or another and you will have days when you just don't want to. I certainly did, and still do. But I can tell you this—as I began to consistently seek God's face, the result was the sweetest and most rewarding fellowship I'd ever had with my Heavenly Father. No earthly relationship has been able to compare. And that's the way He wants it.

I believe God places dreams and passions in our hearts that He wants us to pursue, but *none* of them are as important as the pursuit of Him. In the words of Paul Chappell, "Placing him first in your life should be your daily goal, the main pursuit in the midst of all your other pursuits."[4]

I believe God places dreams and passions in our hearts that He wants us to pursue, but none of them are as important as the pursuit of Him.

CHALK TALK

Player Application

Are you guilty of playing "me ball"? Please understand that on your own, you have limitations. When we submit to God's authority in our lives, He can do immeasurably more than we could ask or imagine, because of his power that is at work within us (Eph. 3:20). If you are willing to commit your life to Christ and pursue Him above all your other passions, I can say with utmost confidence that He will reward your faithfulness in ways you never expected. Have you ever made a personal decision to commit your life to Christ? To pursue Him above anything or anyone else? If you have not or you are unsure, before you go any further in this book, let's take a strategic timeout and discover the "Fundamentals" of the Christian faith beginning on page 17 and deliberately work through those five fundamentals.

Even if you've already surrendered your life to Christ, I'm calling a *team timeout*. Use this as an opportunity to reinforce the truths you already know and to gain *new* truth, knowledge, and understanding of who God is and who He says you are.

I know, fundamentals seem boring, but the best athletes in the world continue to cling tightly to the fundamentals of the sport in which they play. Case in point: In 2014 while I was in a local gym, I got the privilege to watch Xavier Silas practice in preparation for the Washington Wizards training camp. Guess what he was working on? Basic, fundamental ball handling! Down and back, he pounded two balls into the hardwood, working on his handles, pushing himself to do the little things right. Silas went on to be the Wizards third-leading scorer in the preseason that summer before signing a deal in Athens. If professional athletes continue to focus on the fundamentals, why not you?

COACH & PARENT APPLICATION

What about you, coach? Parent? Do you struggle with making Jesus Christ your greatest pursuit? Idolatry is not a youth problem, it's a humanity problem that starts in our hearts. Just this morning, I was having a conversation with my kids about "where our treasure is" and how easy it is to value earthly possessions more than our relationship with Christ. We all agreed that being an authentic Christian is very difficult, no matter what age we are. It requires eliminating the things in our lives that don't really matter and concentrating on the things that do. This is clearly illustrated in Luke 10:38-42 about the lives of two sisters, Martha and Mary. Martha opened up her home for Jesus and His disciples when they were traveling. Mary sat at the Lord's feet listening intently to what He said, but Martha was distracted by all the preparations that had to be made. Martha came to Him and asked, "Lord, don't you care that my sister has left me to do the work by myself? Tell her to help me!" "Martha, Martha," the Lord answered, "you are worried and upset about many things but few things are needed—or indeed only one. Mary has chosen what is better and it will not be taken away from her" (NIV).

Have you chosen what is better? I'll ask you the same question I asked the players: Have you ever chosen to receive Jesus Christ as your Lord and Savior? If you have not, or you're unsure, before you go any further in this book, I am pleading with you to turn to the "Fundamentals," beginning on page 17 and deliberately work through the five fundamentals in their entirety. If you have already given your life to Christ, I want to invite you to return to the "Fundamentals." I know it might seem rudimentary, but basketball legends John Wooden and Phil Jackson were known for being obsessed with fundamentals. Wooden even went so far as to teach his players how to put on their socks and tie their shoes (a lesson some of our kids still need). There is power in the fundamentals, *especially* as they relate to your faith!

PERSONAL TRAINING

I've given you a lot to think about today, so before turning to the "Fundamentals" section, jot down three areas in your life where you could be erecting idols. Feel free to use the list I've provided or add your own. If nothing comes to your mind, then Jesus must be at the forefront of yours. Keep it up!

_____

_____

_____

POST-GAME PRAYER

God, help me to develop a genuine passion for you. Let seeking Your face be the pursuit of my life even when I'm busy, which seems to be always. Teach me how to align my heart with Yours. Help me to discipline my body to wake up early so I may discover the joy that comes from opening the Scriptures first thing each day. And Father, forgive me for putting many things before You. You allow me the freedom to make a choice of where I'll spend my time. I'm glad I chose You today! In the precious name of Jesus I pray. Amen.

CHAPTER 3
FUNDAMENTAL #1
DON'T BELIEVE THE LIES

Jesus answered, "I am the way and the truth and the life.
No one comes to the Father except through me."
John 14:6 (NIV)

FOR JUST A MOMENT WE NEED TO STEP OFF THE
court and use a timeout. Timeouts are called at strategically
important points in the game or when something significant needs
to be communicated to the team. Sometimes the coach has to
deliver some hard truth that is uncomfortable to hear but it's necessary. This is one of those times. However, before you can hear
the truth, you need to know what's not true so you can recognize and distinguish the truth from the lies. I'm talking about the
lies circulating throughout the world with respect to how you can
become a Christian.

Jesus clearly tells us there is *only one way* to God, the Father.
In John 14:6 Jesus says, "I am the way and the truth and the life.
No one comes to the Father except through me." One way. JESUS.
But despite that simple, powerful truth, mankind is misguided
everyday by false beliefs leading them to the conclusion that salvation (deliverance from sin and its consequences) can be achieved
through multiple means. According to the Bible, that is far from
the truth! John 8:44 tells us Satan is a liar and he wants to create
confusion about how we come to Christ. He'll use any means

necessary to keep us from the truth, including religious beliefs that are *almost true*. Listed below are common lies the world accepts as truth, deceiving many people into believing they are Christians.

- *I'm a good person.* Being a good person *does not* make you a Christian nor does doing good works. After all, how much good is good enough? Ephesians 2:8-9 makes this very clear. "For by grace you have been saved through faith. And this is not your own doing; it is the gift of God, not a result of works, so that no one may boast" (ESV). While good works cannot earn you salvation, they are still important and should accompany your faith. What good is it if someone says he has faith but does not have works? Faith by itself, if it does not have works, is dead (Jas. 2:14, 17).

- *I was born a Christian.* For many people around the world, religion is part of their heritage. You can be born Jewish, Muslim or Hindu, but you *cannot* be born Christian. In John 3:3, Jesus said to Nicodemus, a very religious man, "Truly, truly, I say to you, unless one is born again, he will not see the kingdom of God." Nicodemus was baffled at this weird statement, just like you or I would have been, so he asked, "How can someone be born when they are old? Surely they cannot enter their mother's womb a second time to be born." Jesus wasn't talking about a physical rebirth. He was talking about a "spiritual birth." Have you ever heard the phrase, "Born again Christian"? It refers to a change of heart—the new life a person finds when he or she repents of their sins and turns to Christ for salvation. As a result, they become a child of God.
  Many NBA greats such as Dwight Howard, Jeremy Lin, Dwyane Wade, Kevin Durant, Nate Robinson and Steph Curry boldly profess to be born again believers. And that's just to name a few.[5]

- *We are all children of God.* I suppose most people think this is a true statement but the fact is, it's not. All humans are God's creation and we belong to Him because He formed us and created us in His image. But there's a huge difference between being God's creation and God's children. As a human being, you were born into a family and nothing can ever change that. But when you invite Jesus into your heart, you are spiritually reborn into another family—the family of God. When Jesus was in the world, many didn't recognize Him for who He was—the Christ. We are told that even His own people rejected Him. "But to all who did receive him, who believed in his name, he gave the right to become children of God" (John 1:12). God doesn't depend on us to be His children but He wants us to be. He doesn't force Himself on us; He lets us choose. God chose you from the beginning of time because He loves you desperately.

  When Steph Curry was in fourth grade, he *chose* to give his life to Jesus and went from being God's creation to a child of God. In a Fellowship of Christian Athletes article, Curry wrote, "I'm proud to be a child of God. It's in His name that we play and go out and perform and compete and using the gifts He has given us in the right way."[6]

- *Baptism saved me.* All scripture says that people are saved by simple faith in Christ without any act of righteousness, including baptism. Baptism is never mentioned as part of the plan of salvation but was something that accompanied a person's faith in Jesus Christ.

  Numerous scriptures support the fact that people believed first and then were baptized. Mark 16:16 is one of those scriptures: "Whoever believes and is baptized will be saved, but whoever does not believe will be condemned." So being baptized as a baby (or as an adult for that matter), does not make you a Christian. The act of baptizing a baby is more about the parents' decision to begin a life-long journey of faith for their little one. For the child, the decision to follow Christ will hopefully come as he or she grows in their knowledge and understanding of who Jesus is. Once the decision to follow Christ is made, the new believer should follow up with baptism. Baptism does not save you! It's simply an outward sign of an inward decision. In addition, baptism is not an absolute requirement for salvation but Jesus did command it in Matthew 28:19.

On November 18, 2018, The Tennessee Volunteers men's basketball team was in New York City for the NIT Season Tip-off Tournament, but the team took a break from the court for a life-changing moment for Kyle Alexander and Jordan Bowden. The two players took a big step in their Christian faith by getting baptized as their teammates watched. Coach Rick Barnes said what happened with Alexander and Bowden was far more important than any win they'd ever had.[7]

- *Going to church makes me a Christian.* Not true. Christianity is more about living your life for Jesus *day after day* versus sitting in a church pew week after week. Being a follower of Jesus Christ is a lifestyle, not a weekly event. There's a famous saying by Billy Sunday that supports this statement: "Just going to church doesn't make you a Christian any more than standing in a garage makes you a car."[8]

Being a follower of Jesus Christ is a lifestyle, not a weekly event.

It's not uncommon to hear people say, "I don't have to go to church to worship God." That is entirely true! Even so, God's word tells us not to neglect meeting together because we need one another! In Hebrews 10:24-25 we are asked to consider how we might spur one another on and encourage each other toward love and good deeds. This is done by "not giving up meeting together, as some are in the habit of doing."

Like many of you, professional athletes play games on Sundays, which keeps them from attending church services. For that reason, the NBA and WNBA offer pregame chapel so the players can meet together for worship. It takes place sixty minutes before tip-off in every arena, no matter how high the stakes of the game. It's a regular routine for numerous players around the league—stretch, shoot, chapel. Ruth Riley Hunter, now retired from the WNBA states, "Pre-game chapels helped me give God my distractions and focus on His strength."[9]

- *I am not a sinner.* Romans 3:23 says, "for all have sinned and fall short of the glory of God." If that's not clear enough, 1 John 1:8 says, "If we claim to be without sin, we deceive ourselves and the truth is not in us." But what if you've never been shown these scriptures? Would you know you're a sinner?

I vividly recall a day my sophomore year in high school. I was standing in a long hallway between the lunchroom and gym, having a conversation with a fellow classmate when he said the words, "I don't sin." I was shocked and dumbfounded. I suspect he, like many, thought sin only referred to "big things" such as murder, adultery, or stealing; but the reality is *all* sin separates us from God. And because sin separates us from God, we need a Savior to bring us back into right standing with God.

Here's some comforting news: When we choose to receive Jesus Christ as our Savior, we no longer have to be identified as a sinner, but as one who has been made righteous through Jesus Christ's finished work on the cross! As you begin to recognize sin in your own life, you might also begin to recognize the need for Jesus as your Savior. To fully understand our need for Jesus, let's extend our time-out and explore the area of sin in the next chapter. But first, let's take a brief survey:

PERSONAL TRAINING

- Have any of the lies listed in this chapter fooled you into believing you are a Christian?
  Yes _____ No_____
  If you answered "yes," which one(s)?

_____

_____

- After reading this chapter, do you have any concerns about your salvation? If the answer is yes, don't be discouraged. Keep reading!

- According to Scripture, how many ways lead to God? (refer to John 14:6)

_____

POST-GAME PRAYER

Heavenly Father, search my heart. If I have been trying to earn salvation by any means other than through Jesus Christ alone, reveal that to me right now. Your word is clear—*You* are the way, the truth, and the life. No one comes to you except through Jesus. I can't earn my way there. I can't work my way there. I can't perform my way there. I need only to receive Your free gift of grace, believe in the name of Jesus, confess and repent of my sin, and accept my new identity as a child of God. Give me a clear understanding of where I stand with You. As I continue to read the word that is presented, may the eyes of my heart be enlightened in order that I may know the hope to which You have called me, the riches of Your glorious inheritance and Your incomparable great power for those who believe! Amen (Eph. 1:18-19).

CHAPTER 4
FUNDAMENTAL #2
LET'S TALK ABOUT SIN

For all have sinned and fall short of the glory of God.
Romans 3:23 (NIV)

THERE'S NO SENSE IN TALKING ABOUT JESUS IF we don't talk about sin. After all, that's why Jesus came to earth—to save us from our sins! We all sin. I sin, my pastor sins, the Pope sins, even the late Billy Graham was a sinner, and he wasn't afraid to tell you so.

When you hear the word "sin," the Ten Commandments may come to mind. You know, the "major sins" such as murder, adultery, and stealing. We can trick ourselves into believing that it's the really "big" sins that keep us separated from God, but the reality is that *all* sin separates us from God. Isaiah 59:2 (NLT) says, "But your iniquities (sin) have separated you from your God; your sins have hidden his face from you that he will not hear." This doesn't just apply to some people. It applies to all people. Romans 3:23 says, "For all have sinned and fall short of the glory of God."

In the original translation of the Bible, sin literally means "to miss the mark." It's a Greek word that comes from an archery term meaning to miss the bullseye, or in the case of basketball, to miss a shot. Pastor Duke Taber rephrases Romans 3:23 in this way: "All have missed the mark and didn't get their arrow to hit the perfection of God."[10] If you shoot 100 free throws and make ninety-five

24

of them, that's pretty darn good—but not perfect. You still missed. Essentially, even though ninety-five percent of your shots were good you, still made mistakes.

We all mess up. Wouldn't you agree? When you're on the basketball court, you make mistakes. Sometimes, you make the same mistake over and over again. It might be as minor as not making the smartest pass or it could be as major as making the winning basket for the other team. Oh, I've seen it happen! When I was in middle school, one of the most popular guys in my grade experienced the mental and emotional anguish that comes from such a mistake. What made it even worse was that our girls' basketball team witnessed the mortifying moment! Almost forty years later, I still remember it like it was yesterday. I bet he does too.

As much as you don't want to make mistakes, they happen. Eventually, you learn, grow into your game, and mistakes are made less frequently. But rest assured, as long as you're playing basketball, you'll goof up. Your coach messes up, the referees mess up, and your parents even mess up (but you already knew that)! One of the greatest areas of personal growth comes when you can acknowledge your mistakes and then move on.

God wants us to recognize our mistakes too. By acknowledging our sins and showing sorrow for them, we acknowledge our need for Christ's forgiveness. "For the kind of sorrow God wants us to experience leads us away from sin and results in salvation. There's no regret for that kind of sorrow. But worldly sorrow, which lacks repentance, results in spiritual death" (2 Cor. 7:10 NLT).

So what is sin and what does it look like in our everyday lives? Sin is anything we do, say, or think that is not pleasing to God, including our attitude. Some fairly common examples are being prideful, wanting what

> *Sin is anything we do, say, or think that is not pleasing to God, including our attitude.*

25

others have, being self-righteous, judging others, looking at inappropriate material, using profane language, showing disrespect, tearing others down, and being downright mean. And that's just to name a few! You could easily apply this list to your character on or off the basketball court. Have you ever been prideful after playing a great game, shown disrespect to the referees or your coach, or gossiped about a teammate in front of other teammates? Have you ever punched an opponent in the gut when you thought the ref wasn't watching? Yeah, I'm not too proud of that moment. But enough about me! I must confess that sometimes basketball brings out the worst in me. Even now, watching my own kids play, there's an active battleground in my mind. Am I going to publicly criticize the refs when they're calling a one-sided game or am I going to practice self-control and keep my mouth shut? The struggle is real!

Do you get the picture? If you are wondering if you're struggling with a sin issue, just ask yourself, "Would this be pleasing to God?" If the answer is "no," confess your sin the moment you become aware of your sin. Follow up your confession with repentance.

Confession and repentance go hand in hand, but they are two very different things! Confession acknowledges sin. To repent means to turn away from sin and turn to God. It basically means to change your mind. Acts 3:19 says, "Repent, then, and turn to God so that your sins may be wiped out, that times of refreshing may come from the Lord."

Here's an important side note: God may not convict you of something that He convicts me of and vice versa. In my experience, the closer I've grown to Jesus, things that may have been acceptable for me to say or do don't feel right anymore. For example, even though I'm over fifty years old, I have strong convictions about the movies I watch. I was recently watching a film that was rated PG-13 and the language got a little raunchy. Even though no one else was home, I felt very uncomfortable so I chose a different movie. You may not have that same conviction, and that's okay. Therefore, it's important to not judge one another based on our own personal convictions. Ultimately, it's for God to judge our hearts, so let's leave the judging to Him!

While the word "sin" has a negative overtone, once we receive God's free gift of grace, we can celebrate our victory over sin because of what Christ did on the cross! Hebrews 10:10 says, "Our sins are washed away and we are made clean because Christ gave His own body as a gift to God. He did this once for all time." That's right! He took *all* mankind's sin upon himself one time for everyone! One and done! And I'm not referring to the kind of "one and done" that Greg Oden and Kevin Durant faced when they entered the NBA after one year of college ball. To help you fully understand Christ's "one and done," let me briefly explain the incredible significance of Christ's sacrifice on the cross. Don't tune out. This is cool!

In the Old Testament, God's people had to make animal sacrifices in order to experience forgiveness of their sins. This process was known as *atonement*. Once a year, on the Day of Atonement, the high priest was commanded to make an offering of two goats. One goat was sacrificed in order to make atonement for the sins of all the people in the Israelite community. The second goat was a symbol of those sins being removed from God's people. That was the lucky goat—the "scapegoat." The priest would place both hands on the head of the goat, symbolically placing all the sins of the Israelite people on him, but then the goat was released back into the wilderness. This had to be done year after year to keep God's people in right standing with Him. Jesus takes the place of those animal sacrifices! Not only did He sacrifice His body on the cross for you and me, but the weight of all the sins of the world were laid on Him, just like they were laid on the scapegoat; except you and I are the ones that got set free, unscathed. Jesus came to make atonement for our sins *one time* for *all* mankind. That's the kind of one and done that gives you and I forgiveness of our sins *and* eternal life!

Dwight Howard, center for the Houston Rockets, sums up God's gift of forgiveness and the sacrificial love of Jesus Christ in this way: "Everybody needs to realize that it doesn't matter how old you are or how young you are, you still can be a Christian and live for God. It's not easy but that's why we have God's word and He forgives us when we do something we shouldn't be doing. You know, God sent His son to die for us and He paid that sacrifice so you can go to Heaven."[11]

PERSONAL TRAINING

- Sin can be described as anything you do, say, or think that is not pleasing to God, including your attitude. Take a moment to think about areas in your life where you may be experiencing sin, according to our definition. Would you be willing to list a few here?

_____

_____

- God wants us to acknowledge our mistakes by confessing them to Him. Look up 1 John 1:9. What does God say He will do if we confess our sins to Him?

_____

_____

- Is it possible to confess your sin without repenting? Is it possible to repent without confessing your sin? Explain.

_____

_____

POST-GAME PRAYER

Most merciful God, I confess that I have missed the mark of perfection by sinning against You in thought, word, attitude, and action. I have followed the desires of my own heart rather than following You. I have done things I should not have done and have left things undone that I should have done. I am truly sorry and humbly repent. Give me the wisdom necessary to turn away from sin and turn to You, daring not to repeat the same mistakes over and over again. Help me to take delight in Your will and to walk in Your ways. I pray this in the name of Jesus Christ, the one who made atonement for my sins. Amen.

CHAPTER 5
FUNDAMENTAL #3
WHAT EXACTLY IS A CHRISTIAN?

The disciples were first called Christians at Antioch.
Acts 11:26b (NIV)

I WAS RECENTLY AT AN NCAA CERTIFIED BASKET-ball tournament. My daughter's team came up against a solid team from Oklahoma that included a player who was six feet, six inches tall. At first sight, we seemed to be in tall trouble, but once the teams hit the court, it was evident that the expectation we had of her size didn't measure up. No pun intended. We confused her height to mean she was highly skilled, but her minutes on the court proved otherwise.

By the same token, it's easy to look at people who call them-selves "Christian" and upon closer observation be confused about their actions. After all, it's highly likely you have "Christian" friends whose behavior doesn't measure up to what you'd expect from a follower of Christ. Perhaps your expectation of how Christians are *supposed* to behave have been shattered by poor examples.

So what exactly is a Christian? It's a great question, and since the Bible is the authority for the Christian faith, let's see what it has to say about Christians. Here's an interesting fact: The bible only uses the term "Christian" three times!

- "So for a whole year, Barnabas and Saul met with the church and taught great numbers of people. The disciples were first called Christians at Antioch" (Acts 11:26).
- "Then Agrippa said to Paul, 'Do you think that in such a short time you can persuade me to be a Christian?'" (Acts 26:28)
- "However, if you suffer as a Christian, do not be ashamed, but praise God that you bear that name" (1 Pet. 4:16).

The name "Christian" comes from a Greek word meaning "a follower of Christ." It wasn't a term Jesus's disciples gave themselves—it was a name given to them by the people living in Antioch, a city comparable to New York City. As with most nicknames, they're given to you by other people based on your character or behavior. For example, Karl Malone, one of the best power forwards in NBA history, was given the name "Mailman" while at Louisiana Tech because he "always delivered." George Gervin was nicknamed "The Iceman" because he would never sweat (even after a full practice or game) and he always kept his cool on the court. In the same way, "Christian" was a name given to Christ's followers because their behavior and character reflected Christ.

The early Christians believed Jesus to be the *Christos*, meaning "the anointed one" or Messiah. They believed Jesus was the Son of God and that He came to save them from their sins. That is the basic belief of Christians worldwide. What do you believe about Jesus? Do you believe He came to save you from your sins? Do you consider yourself to be a Christian? If not, do you know what you must do to be saved? It's an age-old question. In fact, in Acts 16:30, the jailer assigned to Silas and Paul during their imprisonment asked them, "Sirs, what must I do to be saved?" In other words, *"What must I do to become a Christian?"*

Consider this: What if a young athlete asked, "What must I do to become a professional basketball player?" The answer would likely include a long and exhaustive list of things that would have to be done. The athlete would have to work on those things day after day, year after year, and only *hope* they had done enough to earn their way onto a college roster and possibly play in the NBA or WNBA. Statistics show that only 3.4 percent of male, senior high players end up playing NCAA college basketball—a figure only slightly higher for girls at 4.0 percent. Of those athletes, only 1.3 percent of NCAA male, senior players are drafted into the NBA and only one percent of female players are drafted into the WNBA.[12] So, the likelihood of putting in all that work and *still* not being good enough is a very real probability.

I have some great news! Becoming a Christian is not like becoming a collegiate or professional basketball player. And being saved does not involve a long and exhaustive list of things you have to do. That would be what we call "religion." Religion is full of man-made rules and ceremonies dictating what you have to do in order to be saved. Romans 1:16 says it is the power of God that brings salvation to everyone who believes, not the power of man! In fact, after the jailer asked Paul and Silas what he had to do to be saved, they didn't give him a long to-do list. Instead, they responded with, "Believe in the Lord Jesus and you will be saved..." Really? That's it? You mean we don't have to *work* our way to heaven? No! In fact, you don't have to do *any work* at all! Jesus Christ already did the work for you on the cross!

So then, what *is* required of you? In two words, BELIEVE and RECEIVE. *Believe* the gospel message of Jesus Christ and *receive* His free gift of grace. The gospel (also referred to as the "good news") can be summed up in 1 Corinthians 15:3-4 as recorded by the Apostle Paul: "For what I received I passed on to you as of first importance: that Christ died for our sins according to the Scriptures, that he was buried, that he was raised on the third day according to the Scriptures."

After Jesus was raised from the dead, he appeared to over 500 witnesses. That's a lot of eyewitnesses! So in a sense, we're not just asked to believe in a set of principles taught by the church, but in *real, powerful, historical events* that were witnessed and recorded in ancient documents—events that were exactly as the Scriptures predicted!

So what else do professing Christians believe? Christ-followers believe, *through faith,* that Jesus Christ is the Son of God and that through believing in Him and obeying his Word, we will inherit eternal life. Christians believe that Jesus died for all mankind, paying the penalty for our sin, and that He will come again. Christians believe in the Trinity—God as Father, Son, and Holy Spirit—three distinct persons in one!

The Holy Spirit is a free gift we receive the moment we accept Jesus Christ as our Savior and make him Lord of our lives. The Holy Spirit acts as our counselor, comforter, advocate, guide, teacher, friend, coach and so much more (Matt. 3:17; John 3:16; Rom. 5:8; Heb. 9:28; Eph. 1:13-14; John 14:25-26).

Many people think they must behave a certain way in order to become a Christian or "clean up their act" before they can enter the church doors, but the Bible explains that becoming a Christian is not about behavior but about responding to Jesus's offer of forgiveness. When people are serious about inviting Jesus into their lives, they want to behave differently because their relationship with God changes them from the inside out. Likewise, when athletes are genuinely serious about developing their skills, they don't do things the way they used to. Patterns of practice change, the amount of hours spent in the gym increases, their spirit of determination shifts, and as a result, so does their game. Becoming a great player is an inside-out process as well. It starts deep within the heart. Proof of that commitment and dedication will be evident, just as it is when Jesus does a work in your heart.

Becoming a great player is an inside-out process as well. It starts deep within the heart.

In summary, to become a Christian...

- You must *believe*, in faith, that there is only one true God (Isa. 44:6).
- You must *believe,* in faith, that Jesus is the Son of God (John 1:14).
- You must *believe* that Jesus died for all your sins, was buried and rose from the dead after three days, according to Scripture (1 Cor. 5:3-4).
- You must *believe* that you are a sinner in need of a Savior (Luke 19:10).
- You must *confess* and *repent* of your sins (1 John 1:9).
- You must *receive* Jesus as your Savior. Upon doing so, you become a child of God, and God's children are called to behave differently (John 1:12).
- You are called to *set yourself apart* to be holy, just as God is holy, and to be a light in a dark world (1 Pet. 1:16; Matt. 5:16).

Being set apart from the world doesn't mean you can't have fun! On the contrary, you can still have tons of fun! Nevertheless, we shouldn't participate in the things that go against the nature of God, such as illegal drug use, underage drinking, using profanity, disrespecting teachers and parents, having *any* type of sex outside of marriage, etc. Most assuredly, Jesus died for all those sins, and more! If you have already participated in any of these activities (or in the future), don't lose heart! There is not one sin that Jesus's blood didn't cover on the cross. However, when you come to that moment where you fully surrender your life to Jesus, the desire to do these things should diminish, reflecting your appreciation and love for the great price Jesus Christ paid for you on the cross.

Not only should we set ourselves apart by our lifestyle, but we should set ourselves apart by getting away with Jesus as often as possible to read His Word, spend time in prayer, and allow God an opportunity to speak back. The more often we read biblical truth, the temptation to cave into ungodly temptations becomes less difficult to resist.

Have you ever made a deliberate decision to set yourself apart from the rest of the world by accepting Jesus as the Lord of your life? Romans 10:9 promises, "If you confess with your mouth Jesus as Lord, and believe in your heart that God raised Him from the dead, you will be saved." It's that simple!

I would love to encourage you to start a personal relationship with the One who created you and loves you, *no matter what you've done*, by inviting Him into your life. You can do that by talking to God through prayer. If you aren't sure how to pray, I've included some sample prayers for you in the next chapter. IMPORTANT: there is no such thing as a magic prayer! If you choose to use one of these prayers, please understand it's not the words in the prayer that save you. Only Jesus Christ has the power to save. Salvation is a matter of the heart, not a matter of words.

Salvation is a matter of the heart, not a matter of words.

PERSONAL TRAINING SESSION

- Do you have a nickname? If so, what does it mean and why was it given to you?

_____

_____

- If you consider yourself to be a Christian, do you believe you have reflected Christianity well? If not, what can you do to change that?

_____

_____

_____

- Look up 1 Peter 2:9-10 on being set apart. What has God called you out of?

_____

_____

POST-GAME PRAYER

Most High God, You have called me out of the darkness to give me a new life. You have set me apart for a special purpose and have a divine plan for my life. You have laid the truth of who You are right in front of me. All I have to do is believe it and receive it. Jesus said in John 5:24, "Truly, truly, I say to you, whoever hears my word and believes him who sent me has eternal life. He does not come into judgment, but has passed from death to life" (ESV). Your word leaves no doubt about the decision that is before me. If I have never made the decision to *truly* follow You, lay that on my heart right now. And if I have, may I recommit my heart to follow You as one who has already been given the gift of eternal life—wholeheartedly loving You from this day forward. In Jesus' name I pray. Amen.

CHAPTER 6
FUNDAMENTAL #4
Joining Team Jesus—Responding To the Offer On the Table

AS I WRITE THIS CHAPTER, WE ARE IN THE MIDST of an NCAA Evaluation Period. It's a specific time of year when college coaches are allowed to watch an athlete compete in person or visit their school. Based on the evaluations, coaches can make offers to players whom they think will bring success to their programs in the future. In response, players can accept an offer by making a formal commitment to that program or they can hold out for a better offer. It's all part of the recruitment process.

During the NCAA evaluation period, highly sought after players could be playing in AAU tournaments on opposite sides of the nation, which is why it becomes necessary for assistant coaches, recruiters, and scouts to help in the recruitment process. The overall objective is the same—to woo the highly skilled athletes to their respective basketball program. But ultimately, the athlete has to answer the question: Should I commit or hold out for a better offer that may never come?

I'm like one of those recruiters. My mission? To woo you to the team that has yet to be stopped! There's no reason to hold out for a better offer because the greatest offer you will ever receive is on the table—an offer of a lifetime that will usher you into victory today, tomorrow and forever. You get to decide the outcome. Will you rise up in victory by committing to Christ or will you lie down in defeat without Him? The offer will never be retracted. But why wait? John Wooden, one of the greatest college coaches of all time said this of his faith: "I have always tried to make it clear that basketball is not the ultimate. It is of small importance in comparison to the total life we live. There is only one kind of life that truly wins, and that is the one that places faith in the hands of the Savior."[13] The offer awaits. Will you say yes?

Maybe you don't feel worthy to join "Team Jesus." I can assure you of this: No matter who you are or what you've done, God loves you with a depth of love that you cannot begin to comprehend! The Bible says it's an endless love; beyond measurement. It transcends our understanding. This extravagant love pours into you until you are filled to overflowing with the fullness of God (Eph. 3:17b-19 TPT)!

God wants you on his team! He wants you to experience His love and lead you into victorious living! Your journey of faith begins with a decision and commitment that is made in your heart. If you are ready to begin that journey, share that commitment with Jesus today through prayer. Ultimately, He wants to hear from *your* heart, but I have included some prayers that might help guide you. You may also use the space provided to write your own prayer. Luke 15:10 says, "There is rejoicing in the presence of the angels of God over one sinner who repents." If you make the decision to follow Jesus, I also want to rejoice with you! I invite you to share your decision with me by emailing me at Kari@karikieper.com.

REMEMBER: There is no such thing as a magic prayer! If you choose to use one of these prayers, please understand it's not the words in the prayer that save you. Only Jesus Christ alone has the power to save. Salvation is a matter of the heart, not a matter of words.

POST-GAME VICTORY PRAYERS

Jesus, I believe You are the Son of God, that You died on the cross to rescue me from sin and death and to restore me to the Father. I choose now to turn from my sins, my self-centeredness, and every part of my life that does not please You. I choose You. I give myself to You. I receive Your forgiveness and ask You to take Your rightful place in my life as my Savior and Lord. Come reign in my heart, fill me with Your love and Your life, and help me to become a person who is truly loving—a person like You. Restore me, Jesus. Live in me. Love through me. Thank you, God. In Jesus' name I pray. Amen.[14]

Lord Jesus, for too long I've kept You out of my life. I know I am a sinner and that I cannot save myself. No longer will I close the door when I hear You knocking. By faith I gratefully receive Your gift of salvation. I am ready to trust You as my Lord and Savior. Thank you, Lord Jesus, for coming to earth. I believe You are the Son of God who died on the cross for my sins and rose from the dead on the third day. Thank you for bearing my sins and giving me the gift of eternal life. I believe Your words are true. Come into my heart, Lord Jesus, and be my Savior. Amen.[15]

Dear God, I know I am a sinner and there is nothing I can do to save myself. I confess my complete helplessness to forgive my own sin or to work my way to heaven. At this moment I trust Christ alone as the One who bore my sin when He died on the cross. I believe that He did all that will ever be necessary for me to stand in Your holy presence. I thank you that Christ was raised from the dead as a guarantee of my own resurrection. As best as I can, I now transfer my trust to Him. I am grateful that He has promised to receive me despite my many sins and failures. Father, I take You at Your word. I thank you that I can face death now that You are my Savior. Thank you for the assurance that You will walk with me through the deep valley. Thank you for hearing this prayer. In Jesus' name. Amen.[16]

Father, I know that I have broken Your laws and my sins have separated me from You. I am truly sorry, and now I want to turn away from my past sinful life toward You. Please forgive me, and help me avoid sinning again. I believe that Your son, Jesus Christ died for my sins, was resurrected from the dead, is alive, and hears my prayer. I invite Jesus to become the Lord of my life, to rule and reign in my heart from this day forward. Please send Your Holy Spirit to help me obey You, and to do Your will for the rest of my life. In Jesus' name I pray. Amen.[17]

Dear God, I have come to realize that I have placed other gods before You. I have worshipped things and people instead of the One true God. I confess, with my mouth, that I am a sinner in need of a Savior, not just for today, but for always. Thank you for sending Your Son, Jesus, to die on the cross for me, carrying all my sin and shame on His shoulders so I could be set free from the weight of my mistakes. I accept Your free gift of eternal life through Jesus Christ. I am ready to allow You to control my heart, my decisions, my thinking, and my life. Send Your Holy Spirit to be my coach, my counselor, and my guide. Beginning now, help me to walk in Your ways and to obey the guidelines You have lovingly given through Your Word. In Jesus' name I pray. Amen. (Kari Kieper)

Write your own prayer.

_____

_____

_____

_____

_____

CHAPTER 7
FUNDAMENTAL #5
I'VE MADE A FORMAL COMMITMENT. NOW WHAT?

"Commitment is what transforms a promise into reality."
Abraham Lincoln

JEAN-PAUL SARTRE, A TWENTIETH-CENTURY French philosopher said, "Commitment is an act, not a word."[18] Unfortunately, a *verbal* commitment between a college coach and a student athlete is not a guarantee the coach or athlete will actually act on their word. Verbal commitments are unofficial and the NCAA does not recognize or even track them. Any tweet or story you see of an athlete getting an offer or committing to a school before the signing period of their senior year is considered unofficial.[19]

Aren't you grateful that God's offer of salvation is never retracted? Friend, if you've just prayed to receive Jesus Christ as your Lord and Savior, then today is your signing day! It's official! You are now a child of God (John 1:12)! You've made the best decision of your life! There is no power on earth or in heaven that can separate you from the love of Christ or snatch you out of his hand. He guarantees it (Rom. 8: 38-39; John 10:28)!

On signing day, it's common to have a host of family members, coaches, and friends celebrating around an athlete as he or she signs their letter of intent to play for a particular college program. Well, I can assure you, the angels are celebrating over you right now (Luke 15:10)! While the angels and I take great joy in celebrating over you, I want you to know that your decision to follow Jesus *does not* demand an emotional response from you. You're not expected to feel a certain way other than being grateful for what Jesus has done for you. Whether your decision is accompanied by tears of joy, a heart that is bursting with delight, or you currently feel indifferent, if you truly meant what you prayed, your decision is just as valid and can never be made void!

Committing your life to Jesus Christ is just the beginning of a newly paved road that leads to eternal life in heaven that actually begins *now*. It doesn't mean the road will always be easy and smooth because contrary to what you might think, Christians are not immune to hardship or suffering. However, it does mean you will never walk alone! Your Heavenly Father will be with you every step of the way, whether you're on the mountaintop or in the valley, or somewhere in between, He will never leave your side (Deut. 13:6).

So now what are you supposed to do as a new Christian?

Any good coach knows you can't teach an athlete all there is to know about their respective sport in a short amount of time. It's a lengthy process, and so is living the Christian life. In fact, it's a lifelong process. Therefore, I will only give you five "next steps" to jump-start your new journey of faith.

1. Read the Bible

The number one way God speaks to His people is through His Word, the Holy Bible. It is filled with instruction, encouragement, praise, challenges, direction, guidelines, and hope! God loves us so much that He not only tells us how to live, but we see it demonstrated through the life of Jesus. The Bible is God's love letter to us, and it's just as relevant today as it was when it was written.

- *Before you begin reading, ask God to speak to you.* Pray Psalm 119:34, "Give me an understanding heart, so that I may passionately know and obey your truth" (TPT).
- *Concentrate on what you're reading.* If necessary, place your phone in another room so you won't be distracted by it.
- *Personalize what you're reading.* As you read, substitute your name or personal pronouns such as "I" or "me" into verses so they speak directly to you. For example, "He will cover *me* with his feathers and under his wings, *I* will find refuge; his faithfulness will be *my* shield and rampart" (Psalm 91:4).
- *Keep a journal handy and write down anything important that stands out,* such as scriptures, thoughts, questions, prayers, blessings, and highlights from church sermons.
  If you're picking up a Bible for the first time, the gospels (Matthew, Mark, Luke, and John) are a great place to start. And you can't go wrong with Proverbs or Psalms! Proverbs is filled with great wisdom and teaches you how to interact with others the way God intended. No matter where you start, just start!

2. Talk to God

Just as God *really* does speak to us through His word, He is also *really* listening when we pray. One of the greatest gifts God has given us is the privilege of prayer. We have direct access to God because Jesus removed the barrier between us and God—the barrier that was caused by our sin. Jesus Christ is our mediator; our middleman. "For there is one God and one mediator between God and mankind, the man Christ Jesus" (1 Timothy 2:5 NIV).

It would be irresponsible of me to say there is a "right" way to pray because that is simply not true! However, I suggest that as you bring your cares and concerns to Christ, you sprinkle them with thanksgiving and confession as well. As a mother, it brings me great joy when I hear my children say, "Thank you, mom." In the same way, I believe it delights the Lord when we acknowledge and give thanks for what He's actively doing in our lives. Additionally, while you are now a fully forgiven believer, the fact remains that even though we have been made righteous by the blood of Jesus Christ, we will still encounter sin and should never feel "okay" with it. Therefore we must continually confess and repent of our sins the moment we become aware of them.

There's no secret formula for praying. Prayer is simply talking to God—sharing your heart with Him, just like you would your best friend. He hears our prayers on all occasions—whether we're praying silently, out loud or unable to voice a prayer because we're overwhelmed with grief or anxiety. God just wants to hear from you! A final word on prayer: Never feel like someone else's prayers are more worthy to be heard than yours just because they use "religious" words or pray with great passion. God does not show favoritism (Rom. 2:11)!

3. Get Baptized

Baptism is a lot like getting married and putting on a wedding ring. Whether I wear my ring or not, the fact remains, I'm married. However, wearing the ring publicly is a symbol of my love and commitment to my husband. In the same way, baptism does not save you; rather, it's a symbol of your lifelong commitment to Christ and your willingness to share it publicly. Here are three reasons why you should get baptized after receiving Christ as your Savior and Lord:

- *To declare your commitment.* When athletes commit to a college program, they make a big deal of it; they tweet it and post it in every way imaginable, making their decision public. Baptism is a public declaration about your decision to follow Jesus (I dare you to tweet it or post it). Our faith should be personal, but not private. Baptism is about going public with your faith and telling people about the change that's already happened in you.

> *Our faith should be personal, but not private.*

- *Jesus was baptized and commanded it.* Shortly before Jesus started His ministry on earth, He was baptized by John the Baptist, even though He was not a sinner. Yet He humbled Himself to identify with us and give us an example to follow. If the Son of God pursued baptism, why shouldn't we? Not only did He get baptized, but in Matthew 28:19-20 He commanded all of us to make disciples (students of Jesus), and to baptize them in the name of the Father, Son and Holy Spirit.

- *Baptism is a symbol of what Jesus did for us.* Water baptism is a beautiful picture of what our Lord has done for us. As we are immersed in the water, we are symbolically buried with our Lord. When we are raised out of the water, we are symbolically resurrected, raised to new life in Christ! Water baptism also illustrates the spiritual cleansing we experience when we are saved; just as water cleanses the flesh, so the Holy Spirit cleanses our hearts when we put our faith in Christ. Baptism by immersion can be done in a swimming pool, church baptistry, a river, lake, or even a bathtub!

4. Build Friendships with Other Christians

"Don't team up with those who are unbelievers. How can righteousness be a partner with wickedness? How can light live with darkness?" (2 Cor. 6:14, NLT)

This verse is commonly used in regards to marriage. However, I can't think of any reason why we shouldn't apply this verse as a guideline for our closest friendships. Don't get me wrong. If you have friends who don't believe in God or could care less about Jesus, I'm not encouraging you to ditch them. On the contrary, who needs the message of hope more than them? What I *am* encouraging you to do is to seek out like-minded friends who will help keep you accountable to your new faith in Christ. Here are some key characteristics of authentic Christian friendships:

- *Unconditional Love.* Proverbs 17:17 says a true friend loves at *all* times, not when it's convenient for you. Unconditional love is loving your friend for *who* they are, not for *what* they can do for you. Unconditional love overlooks one another's weaknesses and instead builds one another up according to their needs (Eph. 4:29).
- *Rejoice and mourn with one another.* Romans 12:15 says, "Rejoice with those who rejoice; mourn with those who mourn." A true friend doesn't envy your success but rejoices with you. Conversely, a true friend mourns with the friend who experiences failure. It's what godly friends do. Take the time to celebrate each other's victories but even more importantly, be ever-present during the hardships.
- *Accountability and correction.* "You can trust a friend who wounds you with his honesty but your enemy's pretended flattery comes from his insincerity" (Prov. 27:6 MSG). If you're a good friend, you will gently correct your Christian friend when they're behaving in a manner that is contrary to what God would approve of. On the other hand, you should be willing to accept accountability and correction from a godly friend in return. There's no need to point out minor flaws, but when you see behavior that can cause serious damage to another person or to their own reputation, lovingly point it out.

5. Attend a Bible-Believing Church

When searching for a church home, the most important thing to look for is a pastor who preaches from the Bible! That may sound obvious, but I can assure you, there are plenty of pastors who don't carry a Bible to the pulpit. Here are some tips when trying to find a church that preaches the truth of the gospel:

- *Biblical truth should be preached.* If what you're continually hearing sounds more like motivational speeches, practical how-to guides, or the focus is on prosperity, then the Gospel of Jesus Christ is likely being skirted around. Take the motivational speech for what it's worth but be cautious.
- *Sermons should be inspired from the Bible.* There should always be a chapter and verse mentioned from either the Old or New Testament. The Old Testament is just as relevant as the New Testament, so if the church regularly excludes the Old Testament, be on guard. The "whole counsel of God" should be preached (Acts 20:27).
- *All teaching should be "Christ-centered."* The bible is Christ-centered from Genesis to Revelation, so sermons should be too. The Old Testament records the unfolding of the promise of salvation in Christ and the New Testament reveals how Christ came to fulfill that promise. If sermons aren't consistently pointing toward Jesus, keep searching. One word of caution: Do not look for the "perfect" church because it doesn't exist. All churches are filled with imperfect people so why would any church be perfect?

To recap, your action steps as a new believer are to begin a journey of reading and studying the Bible, praying often, pursue baptism, seek out godly friendships, and find a church that will disciple you and help foster your faith. Remember, the faith journey is lifelong! We will never fully understand the ways and thoughts of God on this side of heaven. According to Proverbs 25:2, "It is God's privilege to conceal things and the king's privilege to discover them." I wonder if God hides things from us so we will diligently seek Him and in turn, make new discoveries about not only Him but also about ourselves; a spiritual game of hide-and-seek, if you will.

While God has reserved the right to conceal *some* things, we do have the benefit of having *much* revealed! "The secret things belong to the LORD our God, but the things revealed belong to us and to our children forever, that we may follow all the words of this law" (Deut. 29:29 NIV). As you begin (or continue) in your journey with Christ, may He richly bless you and reveal to you, and your children for generations to come His love, mercy, grace and goodness! Now go get back in the game!

Perspective

Things turn out best for the people who make
the best out of the way things turn out.
John Wooden

Sometimes God wants us to look at our circumstances
through a new perspective. His perspective.
Renee Swope

If you don't like something, change it; if you can't change it,
change the way you think about it.
Mary Engelbreit

CHAPTER 8
A MATTER OF PERSPECTIVE

So we fix our eyes not on what is seen, but on what is unseen,
since what is seen is temporary, but what is unseen is eternal.
2 Corinthians 4:18 (NIV)

LIFE IS FULL OF CHOICES, PERSPECTIVE BEING one of them. Perspective is a particular attitude toward something; a point of view. Two people can look at the exact same thing and see something totally different. Each person has a different perspective. A common example is the "glass half-empty" or "glass half-full" scenario.

The following is an example of two different perspectives in the same situation: Toward the end of basketball practice one day, our team was divided into two groups and put through some competitive team drills. At the conclusion of each drill, the losing team had to run sprints while the winners cheered them on. Each team had one loss at the end of two drills. For the third and final competition, the head coach announced the losing team would have to run an even greater number of sprints. The battle was on! Both teams gave a great effort, but in the end one team fell short. The winning team celebrated as they made their way to the sideline but their enthusiasm was quickly extinguished when the head coach exclaimed, "*Everyone* get on the line. Let's have *everyone* run." "That's not fair!" one player muttered. She was on the winning team. Her teammate, also on the winning team, said with a smile, "It's okay! Just think of it as a victory lap!"

How's that for perspective? As I looked on, my heart was packed with pride and admiration for her attitude. One player saw the obvious: Her team won, but they still had to run. Not fair! The other player saw what no one else did: *"It's good for me. How could it hurt me? In the long run it will make me stronger."* She didn't see the situation as unfair, nor did she fix her eyes on the additional effort she would have to exert. She saw past that, seeing what was unseen by the rest of the team—extra effort that would only make her a more disciplined player. It boiled down to a matter of perspective.

It's easy to take hold of a victim mentality and begin to wallow in self-pity. We don't take time to think past our circumstances to see how God can use them for our good. It's not natural; but in Romans 8:28, we're told that in *all* things God works for the good of those who love Him, who have been called according to His purpose. If you want to get better at basketball, or *anything* for that matter, then you have to practice, which includes practicing a positive perspective. We need to *practice* looking past what is seen and fix our eyes on what is unseen—attempting to gain an eternal perspective. In doing so, we slowly begin to view life from God's perspective, with the right heart attitude. We find a supporting verse in Romans 5:3-4: "Not only so, but we also glory in our sufferings, because we know that suffering produces perseverance; perseverance, character; and character, hope."

Looking back at our practice situation, you can see how one of the players understood this principle. Since this happened at the tail-end of practice and the players were already gassed, this extra running was going to produce some mild suffering. But this young believer in Christ understood that suffering produces perseverance, perseverance produces character, and character produces hope. That is why she could say with conviction, "Think of it as a victory lap!"

I'll leave you with one final example of a positive and eternal perspective. A dear woman named Donna was attending a women's Bible study at my church when she was diagnosed with cancer. She suffered for quite some time before the Lord ushered her into her heavenly home. But there is something Donna said that is permanently ingrained in my mind. On one of the final days of Donna's earthly life, a nurse popped into her hospital room. Donna's disposition must have been reflecting Christ, as usual. The nurse said, "Oh, Mrs. Roark, your cup is always half-full." Donna replied, "No, my cup is overflowing!" Donna knew she was on her victory lap.

CHALK TALK

Player Application

Does this devotional on perspective give you reason to head into your next practice or game with a new attitude? Does it give you reason to view your daily life from a different perspective? It's not natural to fix our eyes on what is unseen, extending beyond what can be seen. *It takes practice* and it's a lifelong process of *intentionally* looking to view your circumstances from God's perspective. As you mature spiritually, you will find it less challenging, but it will never be completely instinctive. Think of the impact you can have, on and off the court, if you begin to live out of an eternal perspective in your circle of friends. As you are well aware, you will encounter adversity! It's a fact, but faithfully remaining in God's Word will remind you of His promises and that His plans are to prosper you and not to harm you (Jer. 29:11).

Coach Application

One night, after coaching a middle school basketball game, I was feeling defeated. My team was highly competitive but we couldn't seem to pull out the win in the final moments of the game. As I drove home feeling hopeless, a phrase from American filmmaker Alex Kendrick's "I Am Second" video rang in my head. It was a clear and direct word the Lord had given him and it was now speaking to me! "Alex, would you rather have an easier road with less fruit or a harder road with more fruit?"[20] It's something I'll never forget, and a perspective that I desperately needed to hear. It changed everything! It was as if the Lord was handing me an elaborate, golden platter with the words "hard road" served upon it, as he whispered, "Trust me, Kari." The win-loss record wasn't the fruit God had intended to produce. It was spiritual growth in a group of girls who impacted my life forever! All I was seeing was our win-loss record, but at that very moment, I began to have an eternal perspective that reached far beyond our stat line.

Parent Application

Having a positive and eternal perspective is one of the greatest lessons we can teach our children, but in order to teach it, we must live it. Are you currently living with an eternal perspective in mind as you maneuver through life's difficult circumstances? The more we focus on God's words, His promises and the abilities He's given us, the more positive of a perspective we can have. A negative attitude limits our opportunities; a positive perspective increases our confidence which opens the door for greatness. Routinely seek God's Word and you *will* see victory, even in the midst of trials.

> *A negative attitude limits our opportunities; a positive perspective increases our confidence which opens the door for greatness.*

PERSONAL TRAINING SESSION

- Given today's lesson, can you think of a time in your life, on or off the court, when you had the opportunity to view your situation from a different perspective but chose to see what everyone else did? Reflect on how you may have handled that differently now.

- Of the attitudes below, which one would you say best describes you? Are you satisfied with your answer?
  - I'm a *"glass half-empty"* type of person.
  - I'm a *"glass half-full"* type of person.
  - I'm a *"my glass is overflowing"* type of person.

  - Read 2 Corinthians 4:18 again. In your own words, rewrite what this verse is telling you.

_____

_____

_____

POST-GAME PRAYER

Father, You are always faithful, therefore, I must learn to see beyond what my physical eyes can see; beyond what is temporary. I need spiritual eyes to see what others do not see. In order to do that, I need the Holy Spirit in control of my heart and mind. The enemy would love for me to be swallowed up by my challenges, but You call me to stand firm, be courageous, and to take on an eternal perspective, knowing that in the end, the victory has already been won. Help me to see a situation differently today than I would have yesterday. In Jesus' name I pray. Amen!

Help | Defense

Those to whom defense is not important
will have the best seat in the game.
Rick Majerus

Be true to yourself, help others, make each day your
masterpiece, make friendship a fine art, drink deeply
from good books—especially the Bible, build a shelter
against a rainy day, give thanks for your blessings and
pray for guidance everyday.
John Wooden

If you're not talking, you're not playing defense.
Doc Rivers

CHAPTER 9

INFALLIBLE HELP DEFENSE

The Lord is my strength and my defense;
he has become my salvation.
Psalm 118:14 (NIV)

I COULDN'T HELP BUT GIGGLE WHEN I READ THE headline by Jeremiah Budon in an online article he wrote during the 2017 NBA finals between the Golden State Warriors and Cleveland Cavaliers: "New Help Defense: Cavs Scream 'Help!' Whenever They're On Defense." Budon continued, "The Cleveland Cavaliers appear to have revamped their defensive scheme by running a new form of help defense, where they all just constantly scream 'Help!' the entire time they're on defense."[21]

According to Budon, LeBron James, Kevin Love, Kyrie Irving, Tristan Thompson, and J.R. Smith yelled "help" in unison as Steph Curry dribbled the ball up court and passed it to Kevin Durant. They continued to yell as Durant drove toward the basket, then passed it back to Draymond Green for a wide open three-pointer. Despite their best efforts to help one another out, the Golden State offense was more than the Cavs could handle.[22]

Isn't that how life can be? Sometimes our best attempts to help one another prove to be ineffective when circumstances transcend beyond our abilities. Just this week, my friend's husband received the devastating news that his cancer had grown and spread into his bones, lymph nodes, and lungs. The family desperately looked to the doctor for help and healing but they were only met with the recommendation to end all treatments. It was a wretched reminder that no matter how much we may want to help someone, there are situations when the best we can do (and it is the best) is to enter into the presence of God and faithfully pray for our loved ones.

Psalm 46:1 reminds us that God is our refuge and strength, an ever-present help in times of trouble. He is our strength and our defense (Psa. 118:14 NIV). In fact, He should be our first line of defense! Despite your circumstances, no matter how grim, God is faithful! He is completely trustworthy to be your defender and He always has your back. He's your weak-side defender that is never late, never out of position, and always reliable. You can fully trust that when you yell "help" He is already there.

> *He's your weak-side defender that is never late, never out of position, and always reliable.*

In the game of basketball, help defense is only as good as its help defenders. For on-the-ball defenders to aggressively force ball handlers in one direction or the other, they must trust that their teammates will support them if they get beat off the dribble.

It's been interesting to observe my young players throughout the years. When defending the player with the ball, I've noticed a reluctance to *fully* commit to pressuring the ball. That reluctance communicates a message to me, the coach: *"I'm going to play it safe; I don't want to get beat. I don't know if my teammates have my back, so I'm going to sag off my man just in case."* They might as well say, "I lack confidence in myself and I don't fully trust my help."

Friends, Jesus is not only your most trusted teammate, but He's already led you into victory if you've placed your faith and life in His hands. He is your Defender. He is your Help. He gives strength to the weary and increases the power of the weak (Isa. 40:29)! When you need help, He's a very present help in times of trouble. Unlike your teammates, He will never fail you, so you don't have to question His trustworthiness. Don't be afraid to ask Him for help. He wants to help you in the small things as well as big things. He defended you on the cross and He'll continue to defend you until the end.

Because we live in a broken world, hard times will be a common thread in your earthly life. You're going to need help. Don't be too proud to ask your friends and family to help you maneuver through the challenges you face. But more importantly, don't forget to ask your Heavenly Father first. The Lord is your mighty defender, perfect and just in all His ways. He is faithful and true; He does what is right and fair (Deut. 32:4).

I don't want to discount the fact that sometimes, in our finite minds, we may think God is not there or that He is running late. However, in accordance with His Word, we must patiently wait upon Him as we continue to call on Him for help. Here are some verses to encourage you if you are discouraged during the waiting period:

- Wait for the LORD; be strong and let your heart take courage; wait for the LORD (Psalm 27:14 ESV)!
- But as for me, I watch in hope for the LORD; I wait for God my Savior; my God will hear me (Micah 7:7 NIV).
- But if we hope for what we do not yet have, we wait for it patiently (Rom. 8:25 NIV).
- Be strong and courageous. Do not fear or be in dread of them, for it is the LORD your God who goes with you. He will not leave you nor forsake you (Deut. 31:6).

CHALK TALK

Player Application

Let's talk basketball first. Do your teammates and coaches a huge favor. The very second you get beat off the dribble or get held up on a screen, yell "HELP!" You have teammates who will leave their man to help you, but they have to know you need help! Many players are still inexperienced at seeing the ball and seeing their man at the same time, so if you alert them them *loudly* that help is needed, they are more apt to quickly step in.

Secondly, please practice asking for help when you need it. It takes strength to acknowledge that some tasks are bigger than you. In Exodus 18, Moses's father-in-law, Jethro, saw Moses trying to do way too much by himself. He basically said, "What you're doing is not good. You're going to wear yourself out! The work is too heavy for you. You cannot handle it alone. Share the load. Get some help!" And he did exactly what Jethro recommended. Getting help does not make you weak; rather, it's a sign of strength (Exo. 18:13-22).

Coach Application

Coaches need help too! Don't hesitate to ask your team parents to help you. I love what Dick DiVenzio suggests in his book, *Runnin' the Show.* He shares the story of a Duke parent who took a year or two off from work to watch his son play for Coach Krzyzewski. Reportedly, the father became "a pain in the butt." Dick said if he were "Coach K," he would have put a camcorder in the dad's hands and asked him to keep the camera squarely on his son so his performance could be evaluated perfectly.[23] Just the thought of that made me chuckle. Perhaps you have some parents that seem to stir things up a bit. Consider giving them a job that will keep them occupied while serving a purpose for you. It's just a thought. The point is, don't be afraid to ask for help!

Parent Application

Have you been in Moses's sandals before? Overwhelmed by responsibilities? Show your children that parents need help too, and there's no shame in asking for help. Jethro had to point out to Moses that he was doing too much. (I bet Moses knew it). I love the advice Jethro gave Moses in the text: *Teach* them God's decrees and instructions and *show* them the way they are to live and behave.

If I'm being honest, I've passed up countless opportunities to teach and show my children how they could help me with various tasks. My thought process: *It's easier to do it myself.* In the long run, I'm shortchanging them of important life skills and I'm killing myself. That attitude not only demonstrates my need for control, but also my lack of trust. I'm working on this one! I wonder if Moses had control issues? How about you? Could you use some help but aren't willing to ask because you're afraid it won't be done the way *you* want it done? It's very possible our kids might show us a better way of doing something if we simply ask for help.

PERSONAL TRAINING SESSION

- Read Exodus 18:13-22 for yourself. How did Moses's delegation of responsibilities help him? How do you think it helped others?

_____

_____

- Do you have a hard time asking for and accepting help? If you answered yes, why do you think this is so?

_____

_____

- Psalm 46:1 is a powerful verse. Read it and try to commit it to memory today and for a lifetime.

POST-GAME PRAYER

Almighty God, I am thankful that *You* are my strength and my defense, a very present help in time of trouble. I can easily become overwhelmed with my responsibilities, resulting in an anxious spirit. May I recall the words of Psalm 46:1 when I begin to feel worried. Help me to set aside my pride and ask for help when I need it. Thank you for being my Defender now and forever. Help me be a good teammate, supporting my friends when they need help on and off the court, showing myself to be trustworthy and faithful, just as You are. In Jesus' powerful name I pray. Amen!

Building Others Up

If you want to lift yourself up, lift up someone else.
Booker T. Washington

No man can do me a truer kindness in this
world than to pray for me.
Charles Spurgeon

Be one who nurtures and builds. Be one who
has an understanding and forgiving heart;
one who looks for the best in people.
Leave people better than you found them.
Marvin J. Ashton

CHAPTER 10

HEAVY LIFTING IS LIGHT WORK

Humble yourselves before the Lord and he will lift you up.
James 4:10 (NIV)

IN THE WINTER OF 2017, MY SON WAS PLAYING for his high school freshman basketball team. His coach, a recent college graduate and first-year teacher, was young and inexperienced. For a family who had been in the club basketball circuit for several years, his inexperience was frustrating at times. His coaching decisions often had parents shaking their heads. One night in particular, our team was down 5-21, so he subbed in a second-string player who proceeded to hit three three-pointers in a row, quickly bringing the score to 14-21. Finally, we began to feel a sense of hope...until the coach took that player back out of the game. The player approached the bench in tears, frustrated and confused about the substitution. After some equally baffled parents demonstrated their own frustrations, the coach put the player back in. This hot-hand went on to have an incredible performance, and we ended up easily winning the game. I wish I could say this was an isolated incident, but it wasn't. If it hadn't been so infuriating, it might have even been comical.

Not long after that game, I was catching up with a friend from my kids' former school. She asked how my kids were doing and how their transition to public school had been. I shared about my daughter's academic and basketball experiences at her new middle school thus far, then did the same for my son. I proceeded to share my frustrations regarding my son's new basketball coach, and she asked me a very pointed question: "Well, have you prayed for the coach?" "Well, uhhh, no, actually, I haven't," I stuttered. Her question stuck with me. In fact, it kind of stuck me right in the heart!

Later that morning, after reflecting on our conversation, conviction drove me to pray for the coach. In a genuine and fervent prayer, I confessed that I had participated in tearing down the coach rather than building him up, and that I had laughed at and contributed to the remarks parents would make in the stands. I asked the Lord to bless the coach with wisdom and understanding as he coached the game later that day. I also asked the Lord to help him to know *what* to do and *when* to do it. My heart and soul felt better—cleansed from unrighteousness, and grateful to intercede on the coach's behalf. It was just that easy to lift him up—light work!

After the prayer, I texted my son at school. "The Lord gave me a huge revelation just now. I asked Him to forgive me for being ugly about coach. I asked Him to cleanse my heart of all that, and I prayed blessings over him. I want to encourage you to do the same so that it may free the Lord up to work in you tonight. Love you, son." He responded, "Love you, too, and yes, ma'am."

As I entered the opponent's gym that evening, I narrowly missed the tip-off but got to see the first score of the game. It was my son. He hit a beautiful three-pointer from the right baseline. Nothing but net. As the game progressed, he hit another three, then another, and another, and another. By the end of the third quarter, he was eight for nine from the three-point line and three for three from the lane. In all, he had thirty points that night. He was eleven of twelve from the field (without stepping foot on the court in the fourth quarter). As I watched this unfold before my eyes, I *knew* why my son was creating his own highlight reel. It was to highlight what the Lord can do in and through us when we humble ourselves and lift others up. Not only did the Lord bless my son that night, but I was equally blessed.

I had the opportunity to share this humbling testimony several times that week, and I still share it to this day. It continues to serve as a reminder that lifting others up is not only a blessing to them, but to us as well.

We are really good at criticizing our coaches, aren't we? Many spectators want to coach from the sidelines, myself included. I hadn't given *any* thought to the fears, insecurities, criticism, and judgment my son's coach was facing as he mustered up the courage to coach his first-ever high school basketball team. And as if coaching isn't hard enough on its own, the fans, players, and parents can make it even more difficult.

As a coach, I've experienced two extremes: On one particular occasion, I had a parent directly behind my bench, coaching his kid over my shoulder. Not only did it stress me out, but the player was in tears, confused about who to listen to. I've also experienced the other extreme: I've been keenly aware of parents who were quietly supporting me through persistent prayer and encouraging texts and emails. If my son's coach had to choose one experience over the other, there's no doubt he'd choose the supportive, praying parent, the same way we all would.

"Humble yourselves before the Lord, and He will lift you up. Brothers and sisters, do not slander one another" (James 4:10-11a).

CHALK TALK

Player Application

Slandering a coach in front of your teammates is tempting because you will most likely have teammates agreeing with you, taking your side, and contributing to the conversation. But God's Word is clear. We are not to slander one another. The next time your team is roasting your coach, refuse to be a part of the banter, or better yet, steer the conversation in a more positive direction.

Coach Application

As a coach, criticism and judgment come with the territory. It's a tough battle, especially if you're not experiencing a winning season. Let me encourage you to enlist someone to pray for you.

When you become more concerned with pleasing the parents, you lose the ability to focus on your real objective—teaching your players the game.

Keep the following scripture in mind: "The fear of human opinion disables; trusting in God protects you from that" (Prov. 29:25 MSG). Don't let your insecurities get the best of you. When you become more concerned with pleasing the parents, you lose the ability to focus on your real objective—teaching your players the game.

Parent Application

I would like to encourage you to pray for your player's coach, but first, check the motives behind your prayer. If you have been like me (contributing to negative chatter), then confess it to the Lord and turn your grumbling into prayers. Pray in a way that would edify the coach. You can't go wrong if you pray for wisdom and discernment on their behalf.

PERSONAL TRAINING SESSION

- Think of *all* the ways praying for your coach might help him/her *and* your team. List some of those ways below (don't be afraid to think outside the box).

_____

_____

- James 4:10 says the Lord will lift you up when you humble yourself. "Humble" means "having or showing a modest or low estimate of one's own importance." Notice it does *not* say a "low self-esteem," but a "low estimate." Take time to ponder what that means. What does the Lord say he will do if you humble yourself?

- Read Ephesians 4:29. According to this verse, what positive attributes should our speech have?
  - A. It should be _____.
  - B. It should _____ others up.
  - C. It should _____ those who listen.

POST-GAME PRAYER

Father, if I have been guilty of tearing down my teammates or coach, purify my heart of this senseless chatter and remind my heart of James 4:10 and Ephesians 4:29. Help me to remember that my coach and teammates are continually learning, just like I am, and we could all benefit from the act of praying. Let it begin with me. In Jesus' name I pray. Amen.

Availability

God doesn't use great people;
God uses available people to do great things.
Dylan Dodson

Basketball is one of those rare opportunities
where you can make a difference not only for
yourself, but for other people as well.
Bill Walton

Never mistake motion for action.
Ernest Hemingway

CHAPTER 11
HOW'S YOUR AVAILABILITY?

Then I heard the voice of the Lord saying, "Whom shall I send?
And who will go for us?" And I said, "Here am I. Send me!"
Isaiah 6:8 (NIV)

NOTHING DERAILS A MOTION OFFENSE MORE than players standing around waiting to see what the person with the ball is going to do. A motion offense relies heavily on all players being active—passing, cutting, and screening in order to create an open shot or layup. When players aren't in motion, they're easy to guard and difficult to be passed to. As a result, they miss out on scoring opportunities because they haven't made themselves available to the passer and the ball.

In his book, *Stuff Good Players Should Know*, Dick DeVenzio says, "One of the chief assets of a good player that the average fan rarely even considers, and which even the average player rarely considers, is the ability to play the game constantly available to the ball. A player who is constantly available defuses a lot of potentially troublesome situations and prevents a lot of teammates' turnovers. Good players ask themselves constantly, 'Can the ball be thrown to me with no problem?'"[24] Essentially, "Am I available?"

Have you ever called a friend and it went straight to voicemail? You may have heard, "I'm not available to take your call. Please leave a message after the tone." Just because they didn't answer doesn't mean they weren't called. Perhaps your friend had better things to do and declined the call. Maybe they were distracted and didn't hear the call. Or maybe their phone was on "do not disturb,"

71

completely unaware of the call. The fact remains, they weren't available. This leads me to an important question: How available are *you* when God calls? Have you ever felt as if God was calling you to do something and you dismissed the call? I have. I've felt a strong urge in my spirit to speak with someone or act on something and I neglected to do it. Whatever my reason, I was disobedient, and in my disobedience I made myself unavailable to God, therefore, ineffective.

In Isaiah 6:8, God asks the question, "Who shall I send? And who will go for us?" Without hesitation, Isaiah shouted out, "Here am I! Send me." The mission God was sending him on was not an easy one. He had to deliver the news to the Jewish people of their upcoming destruction and doom. Nevertheless, he eagerly volunteered to step out and be sent. Are you willing to step out for the Lord? Stepping out requires action. You can't stand around, observing, if you want to be an active participant for Jesus—a player who's not just wearing a jersey but actively competing in the game.

When you get a stirring in your heart to reach out to someone who's hurting, being mistreated, or seems discouraged, act on your conviction. Make yourself available. When you notice your mom, dad, or guardian scurrying about, trying to manage all the duties of the home, make yourself available by simply asking the question, "Is there anything I can do to help you?" And if the answer "yes," then it's because your help is truly needed. I know! It may not be the answer you were hoping for but pitch in anyway without making a big deal of it.

A final word about being available. A few years ago, I was driving my kids home from school. A grungy, middle-aged man was on the corner of a busy intersection panhandling. I didn't have any cash, but on this particular day I rolled down my window anyway and said, "I'm sorry, I don't have any money; I just wanted to say hello." While he was a man of meager means, his response was astonishing. "Oh, that's okay," he said. "I just want to be recognized." Wow! He simply wanted someone to acknowledge his existence; to be seen! I hope the effortless act of making myself available to simply say hello blessed his day as much as he blessed mine. Being available for others means being available for Christ. "Truly I tell you, whatever you did for one of the least of these brothers and sisters of mine, you did for me" (Matt. 25:40).

CHALK TALK

Player Application

From a coach's perspective, let me give you a tip: Be an *active* player, constantly available to the ball, your teammates, and your coach. Don't just be active with your body; be an active communicator as well! Players who spectate on the court, rather than moving continually, are not nearly as effective as the players who are always in motion. Yes, there are offenses that require you to stand still and wait for screens or appear like you're not in the play, but eventually, *BAM*, you make a fierce cut to the basket for the score. The same goes for your spiritual walk. Are you actively pursuing a deeper walk with Christ? Do you participate in activities that will build your relationship with Him? Being a devoted follower of Christ requires action. It requires being available for Christ when He calls you to step out. It requires *doing*. Make sure your soul isn't on "do not disturb."

Make sure your soul isn't on "do not disturb."

Coach Application

It was early spring in 2018 and my daughter was having a rough day at school. During track practice her coach could tell she wasn't quite herself. The coach put her arm around her and tried to comfort her and make her laugh. When my daughter told me of the incident, I was so grateful to the coach for being available to my daughter. The coach noticed she was upset but didn't dismiss it as teen drama. Are you available to your players when you notice they're not quite themselves? Sometimes, just an arm around their shoulder can be a great comfort. Being available to your players, not just as a coach, but as a mentor and cheerleader can make a world of difference to a child who is discouraged or simply having a bad day.

Parent Application

Are your days filled with activity after activity? The more activities we have lined up, the less time we have together as a family. Let me encourage you to take time for your children—*quality time*—even if you don't think your child wants to spend time with you. Create space together outside of basketball. Invest time to find out what's going on in your child's world, which looks quite different than our world! Whether they want to believe it or not, our children *need* us. Are you too busy or are you able to say, "Here am I?"

PERSONAL TRAINING SESSION

- Consider this quote by Neal A. Maxwell: "God does not begin by asking us about our *ability* but only about our *availability*, and if we then prove our *dependability*, He will increase our *capability*."[25] Take a moment to meditate on the meaning of this quote.

- How does this quote apply to you as a basketball player?

_____

_____

- How can you apply this quote to your spiritual walk with Jesus?

_____

_____

POST-GAME PRAYER

Father, I acknowledge that having a heart like Isaiah, who was willing to say, "Here am I! Send me," is a daunting thought. As I rely less on myself and more on You, I will become more willing to step out in a courageous and bold faith, making myself available to be used by You. I don't want to be ineffective as a Christian or a player. Empower me to be intentionally active, whether I'm playing basketball or living out my daily life. I want to be used by You so I can magnify the name of Jesus Christ. Amen.

Respect

Respect for ourselves guides our morals;
respect for others guides our manners.
Laurence Sterne

I don't mind a guy going at me at both ends of the floor,
I can respect that. But when guys start throwing elbows and
when they kick you when you're down, that's
dirty basketball and I don't respect guys like that.
Ray Allen

Maturity is developed by respecting others and
accepting responsibility for violating that respect.
Wes Fesler

CHAPTER 12

RESPECTING AUTHORITY—IT REALLY IS BLACK AND WHITE

*Have confidence in your leaders
and submit to their authority,
because they keep watch over you
as those who must give an account.
Do this so that their work will be a joy,
not a burden, for that would be of no benefit to you.*
Hebrews 13:17 (NIV)

THIS LESSON IS A HARD ONE TO TEACH, AND AN even harder one to apply. Why? Because we are talking about authority in our lives, *including referees*. A referee, or "ref," is a person of authority who is responsible for officiating a game from a neutral point of view. Referees make decisions that enforce the rules of the game, including violations, fouls, and ejections. Of equal importance, referees are responsible for ensuring the safety of the players by maintaining order on the court throughout the game.

From the coaching box, there were days when I would shake the ref's hand for a job well done, and other days when I felt like our opponent *was* the ref. It's fair to say that throughout the years, I've given my fair share of criticism to referees. Interestingly enough, as much as I argued or complained (even if I was right), I've never had a call reversed. Despite the fact that referees are *supposed* to call the game from a neutral stance, I don't always see it that way. And even though refs are *supposed* to keep players safe, I've watched referees allow the game to get overly physical and out of control. Add to that the inconsistency of the calls and it makes for some highly emotional players, coaches, and parents. For this reason, their authority is subject to all kinds of ridicule. They get cursed at, harassed, and on rare occasions even physically attacked. It's no wonder there's a shortage of qualified referees. Who wants to sign up for a job like that? Journalist Jonathan Liew puts it this way: "Referees, like politicians, come in two varieties: despicable ones, and the ones you haven't heard of yet. This, I reckon, is the real reason they have traditionally worn black."[26]

Obviously, the best way to deal with a referee during competition is with respect, but how do you deal with referees when there's a plethora of bad calls or they're neglecting calls altogether, even while kids are getting hurt? How do we respond when we see a player or team being victimized? How are we called to respect that kind of authority figure?

According to scripture, it's black and white. In Hebrews 13:17, the Apostle Paul writes, "Have confidence in your leaders and submit to their authority, because they keep watch over you as those who must give an account. Do this so that their work will be a joy, not a burden, for that would be of no benefit to you." In Romans 13:1 he again states, "Let everyone be subject to the governing authorities, for there is no authority except that which God has established. The authorities that exist have been established by God." The first verse has to do with religious leaders and the second verse has to do with government leaders. While referees are not religious or governmental authorities, they still have a place of authority over you, your coach, and the fans.

An example of how we can apply these scriptures is found in 1 Samuel 24. David was anointed to be the next king of Israel but King Saul wanted to kill him because he was a threat to his throne. David was hiding from Saul deep in a cave when, lo and behold, Saul entered that very cave to "relieve himself" (most commentators agree the king was napping, relieving himself from the hot sun, not from a full bladder. Either way, he was a sitting duck). At that very moment, King Saul was in David's grasp and so was the crown! He could have easily killed Saul, but David spared his life. David declares to King Saul in 1 Samuel 24:10, "Some urged me to kill you, but I spared you; I said, 'I will not lay my hand on my lord, because he is the Lord's anointed.'" David wasn't ruled by his emotions. He allowed the principle of respecting God's authority to guide him. He knew that if God wanted him to be king at that time, He would have made him king. Until then, King Saul was David's authority. Why did David respect Saul's position of authority? Because of his love for God.

Our respect for authority is a mirror image of our respect toward God. Whether we agree or disagree with our authorities (religious, polit- ical or otherwise), showing honor and respect is a way we can honor God, and *I believe* this also includes

> *Our respect for authority is a mirror image of our respect toward God.*

referees. You can act respectfully towards a person even if you don't respect them. How is this possible? Because respecting others has to do with *your* character and being worthy of respect has to do with theirs.

If I were to rewrite Hebrews 13:17 to speak to basketball players, it might read something like this: "Have confidence in the referees and respect their authority because they are trying to keep a close watch on the game and keep you safe. After all, they will be judged on their performance. Respect and show them honor so that their job is a joy, not a burden. Besides, if you show a lack of respect, you are not doing your team any favors and it's certainly not a benefit to you or your coach."

Keep this in mind: A referee's job is much more difficult than you might think. They have to make split-second decisions and whether they make the right call or not, it will be the wrong call for someone! According to a referee named Tom, "Being a referee is hard. Let's put that right out there. You are signing up for a job where the expectation is that you will get yelled at, often unjustifiably, and you're supposed to not react and continue to do your job. It is the hardest job I have ever had and may ever have."[27]

CHALK TALK

Player Application

The next time you step on the floor for tip-off, take the opportunity to shake the ref's hand *before* the game. Determine in your mind, *before the game starts*, that if the ref makes a call against you, you will accept the call, *no matter what*, and move on! Let the coach fight for you if he/she thinks it's necessary. Remind yourself you don't have to respect the person calling the game but you are called to respect the position. In doing so, you are honoring God. Additionally, respecting authority says volumes about your character! Be the leader on your team who demonstrates honor and respect.

Coach Application

A terrible call was made in a game. Six players started kicking and punching the referee. A spectator said to the other referee, "Aren't you going to help?" The other ref replied, "No, six should be enough."[28] That joke would be funny if it wasn't a reality. I watched a YouTube video of an AAU team (coaches and players), savagely beat down three referees in an all-out brawl in a tournament in the summer of 2018.[29] And for what? I don't know for certain, but I'm going to assume from the video's comment section that the players and coaches weren't happy with the calls being made. Just as you make coaching errors (and you do), referees make errors too. It's inevitable! But in the end, officials *do not* determine who wins and loses games. The best teams (which usually have the most skilled players) win the games they deserve to win. If you think certain games boil down to the referees' mistakes, then look at your game footage very carefully and see if your team may have made any mistakes that could have cost you the game. The referees aren't the ones who missed those layups or free throws.

Parent Application

Respecting the authority of referees could possibly be harder for you than the players and coaches because your child's safety is in their hands. Generally speaking, we have not done a great job setting an example for our kids when it comes to how we respond to the refs. When parents yell at the refs (myself included), it not only shows parents in a negative light but it can be embarrassing for our children. There's a basic piece of advice we've given our kids from a very young age that our parents gave us: "If you don't have anything nice to say, don't say anything at all." It's so simple, *yet so hard.* Next time the refs make a horrible call, *and they will,* make a determination beforehand that it won't surprise you nor exasperate you. Resist the temptation to vocalize your objections. It will be more beneficial for the team, coach, and your player!

PERSONAL TRAINING SESSION

- Read Romans 13:1-5. How can you apply these passages on submitting to governing authorities to your life on and off the court?

_____

_____

_____

_____

- Are you guilty of questioning the authority of your coach or referees? If so, what can you do to immediately change that behavior?

_____

_____

- According to today's text, how is it possible to respond respectfully to a person even if you don't respect them?

_____

_____

POST-GAME PRAYER

Father, You are my ultimate authority. You have called me to submit to the elders and governing authorities in my life, *unless* they're directing me to sin or do something outside of Your will. I confess that submitting to authority can be challenging, and that includes respecting referees. Help me to honor their position out of respect for You. In doing so, I am given an opportunity to reflect Your character. I cannot do this in my own strength; therefore, Holy Spirit, help me to humble myself by being a player of noble character as I show respect to my coach, opponents, referees, and most importantly, You. In Jesus' name I pray. Amen.

Composure vs. Pressure

Nothing gives one person so much advantage over another
as to remain always cool and unruffled under all circumstances.
Thomas Jefferson

Everything negative—pressure, challenges—is all
an opportunity for me to rise.
Kobe Bryant

You can measure a man's character by the
choices he makes under pressure.
Sir Winston Churchill

CHAPTER 13

COMPOSURE VS. PRESSURE

We are hard pressed on every side,
but not crushed; perplexed, but not in despair;
2 Corinthians 4:8 (NIV)

WHEN A REPORTER ASKED GOLDEN STATE Warrior Stephen Curry how he managed to score one-on-one against Cleveland Cavalier LeBron James in game two of the 2017 NBA Finals, Curry explained: "Honestly, I was rushing to begin with because I felt like there was an angle here or an angle there and there wasn't 'cause there was a huge (defensive) crowd around the right side of the floor. I was able to kind of reset back behind the three-point line. You kind of just give a little hesitation, making him think you're going to shoot, and then you just try and go around him. At that point, I was a little more composed than earlier in that possession—I was like a chicken with my head cut off, running in circles."[30]

Before the game was over, that single possession had already made the highlight reels. It was razzle-dazzle at its finest! Curry can make scoring look easy, but this possession was different. There was intense pressure from the three-time NBA Finals MVP, James, before Curry composed himself enough to score on the six-foot-eight-inch forward. The key to Curry's attack was *composure*. Before he was able to finish at the rim, he was literally running in circles, keeping spectators in suspense as to how he was getting out of this one-on-one battle.

Life is full of pressure and it comes from many different angles. There's no escaping it. Youth deal with peer pressure, academic pressure, parental pressure, pressure to keep their minds and bodies pure, and pressure to live a life of holiness when the enemy wants nothing more than for us to conform to the pattern of this world. As the Apostle Paul puts it, we are hard-pressed on every side; perplexed. But as Christians, we don't have to be crushed or in despair!

In terms of basketball, "press" is short for pressure. Teams press to create pressure for their opponent in hopes they will lose their composure and turn over the ball; and many times it works. It takes a well-disciplined team to handle the pressure of an opponent that runs a solid press. Like Curry, sometimes we have to press the reset button in our minds in order to regain our composure and break through the pressure. It's a physical and mental battle you must prepare for well in advance. That's why teams practice a press break—a counteract to the pressure. Consistently practicing a press break will reduce the likelihood of buckling under pressure because players know *in advance* what moves to make, what options are before them, and the smartest way to advance the ball down the court. It's all part of the game plan.

> *Like Curry, sometimes we have to press the reset button in our minds in order to regain our composure and break through the pressure.*

In the same way that wise coaches teach their teams to respond to defensive pressure in a game, we must also prepare ourselves to handle the pressures that will undoubtedly come our way in the game of life. If we don't prepare and practice how we will respond to the pressure, we could easily crumble in stressful situations. In Philippians 1:27, the Apostle Paul says to the deacons and overseers of the church at Philippi, "Whatever happens, conduct yourselves in a manner worthy of the gospel of Christ. Then, whether I come and see you or only hear about you in my absence, I will know that you stand firm in the one Spirit, striving together as one for the faith of the gospel without being frightened in any way by those who oppose you."

In other words, be so rooted in your faith that despite opposition or persecution, you will conduct yourself in a manner that is consistent with biblical principles. Paul knew persecution toward Christians was inevitable, which is why he told them to stand firm, in one Spirit, striving together. Paul experienced what it meant to be hard-pressed on every side. He experienced oppression, distress, brutal beatings, sleepless nights, hunger, and imprisonment; but despite all that, he never caved into the constant pressure. Hard-pressed? Yes. But crushed? No. In fact, in Acts 16:25, we are told that Paul and Silas prayed and sang songs to God while the other prisoners were listening to them. While Paul certainly may have been perplexed, he was not in despair. He never lost hope, nor was he in distress, discouraged, or in anguish. He knew everything that happened to him was to advance the gospel of Jesus Christ.

What about you? When the basketball is inbounded to you and two opponents thrust toward you for a trap, do you freak out and cave in to the pressure, trying to get rid of the ball like a hot potato? Do you automatically dribble towards the sideline making yourself an easy target for a sideline trap? Do you make careless passes straight into the hands of the opposition because you've lost your cool? What about in your personal life? Can you stand up to the traps that Satan is baiting you for? At every turn, your opponent, the devil, is prowling around like a roaring lion looking for someone to devour (1 Pet. 5:8). You must prepare yourself to respond in a way that is worthy of the gospel of Jesus Christ. As you learn to compose yourself under pressure, not only will you and your team become more successful in advancing the basketball, but you will also be advancing the Kingdom of God as you learn to respond with grace.

CHALK TALK

Player Application

Whether you're playing basketball or going about your daily activities, when pressure comes your way you have to play it cool. Believe it or not, going through pressure situations is actually good for you. As a player, you learn how to deal with pressure by experiencing it and figuring out how to work through it. As a Christian, you have an opportunity to mature through your trials and suffering. There is no hope of reaching the goal of spiritual maturity apart from going through hardships, setbacks, and severe testing and learning how to respond properly. Satan's purpose is to defeat us, but God's purpose in allowing tough times is to bring us to maturity so we can bring glory to Him.[31]

Coach Application

Without a doubt, you routinely experience pressure as a coach! You're responsible for drawing up the game-winning play or arranging your defense to hold off a game-winning shot, all the while keeping your cool so players don't sense your anxiety. Experienced coaches have learned from their past mistakes and are better equipped to deal with high-pressure situations, but probably not before making some bad decisions. Down the road, those previous experiences become a benefit to you; when pressure situations arise, you are more fit to deal with them. Play calling becomes easier because you've practiced, *beforehand,* how to handle the pressure. Are you as prepared to handle life's daily blows? What counteracts do you have for Satan?

Parent Application

How would your child say you respond to pressure, stress, trials, and times of testing? Are you a good example of keeping your composure, allowing the Lord to rule your heart and mind? When tough times come, is your natural inclination to enter into prayer or allow fear to overwhelm you? In 2 Corinthians 4:8-9, Paul says we are afflicted, perplexed, persecuted, and struck down. But he also says what we are *not*. We are *not* crushed. We are *not* driven to despair. We are *not* forsaken. We are *not* destroyed. How is that possible? Paul answers this question in verse 17: "For our light and momentary troubles are achieving for us an eternal glory that far outweighs them all." And that's the prize we must keep our eyes on!

PERSONAL TRAINING SESSION

- On a scale from 1 to 10, how would you rate yourself when it comes to handling pressure situations? 1 = I cave under pressure. 10 = I'm as cool as a cucumber. _____

- Going through times of suffering is difficult and inevitable. What does Paul say about our suffering in Romans 8:18?

_____

- There is no doubt that life's pressures bring about suffering. However, we *can* rejoice in our suffering. Read Romans 5:3-5 and explain how this can be true.

_____

_____

_____

POST-GAME PRAYER

Father, You are a good God, and despite tough times that come my way, You are faithful. Therefore, I will learn to trust You more and more no matter how hard-pressed I am. According to Your Word, You have not given me a spirit of fear and timidity, but of power and love and of sound judgment (2 Tim. 1:7). I confess there have been many times when I've crumbled under pressure and made my circumstances bigger than my God. Help me to remember that even through affliction or despair, I am not crushed, abandoned, or destroyed because of the power that lives in me through the gift of the Holy Spirit. In all things, help me to compose myself in a manner that is worthy of the gospel of Jesus Christ. Amen!

Denial

Satan says, "If you follow me, do what you want."
Jesus says, "If you follow me, deny yourself."
Unknown

The greatest single cause of atheism in the world today
is Christians who acknowledge Jesus with their lips and
walk out the door and deny Him by their lifestyle. That is
what an unbelieving world simply finds unbelievable.
Brennan Manning

God is a presence that I can never define
but I could never deny.
John Shelby Spong

CHAPTER 14
DENYING YOUR MAN

But whoever denies me before men,
I also will deny him before my Father who is in heaven.
Matthew 10:33 (ESV)

"DENY! DENY! DENY!" WHEN YOU HEAR THOSE words being shouted from your coach, you know it means to clog the passing lane and prevent the opponent you're guarding from getting the ball. If your man is one pass away, you know to place your foot and hand nearest the ball slightly forward, and turn the palm of your hand toward the ball so you can deflect or intercept any incoming passes. And you know if the ball-handler picks up their dribble, you have a dead ball situation and everyone should closeout on their man in full-denial, right in their "bubble."

The fundamental skill of being able to deny an offensive player the ball is one of the most important concepts a good defensive player will have. An offensive player cannot score if they don't have the ball. The simple goal of deny defense is this: Do not let the man you're guarding receive the ball. A common line of thought is this: *"If my man gets the ball, I must keep him from scoring."* However, what if you thought, *"I'm not going to let my man even touch the ball so I don't have to worry about him scoring!"* What difference would that make?

"Deny" means "to refuse to give or grant something desired to someone."[32] Additionally, it means "to decline, reject or refuse something."[33] Clearly, that "something" is the basketball. For the defensive player, denying your opponent the ball is effective for your team. For the offensive player, a defensive player denying you the ball is frustrating and makes the game a challenge!

Now let's turn our thinking to spiritual matters. Using that same definition of deny, let's apply it to our focal verse, Matthew 10:33. "But whoever denies (rejects, refuses, declines) me before men, I will also deny before my Father who is in heaven." Of all the great things we know of the Apostle Peter, he is also well-known for denying Jesus Christ. In Matthew 26:34, Jesus told Peter that before the rooster crowed that evening, he would deny him three times. And sure enough, in Matthew 26:70-72, Peter flat-out denied that he even knew who Jesus was! It breaks my heart when I read the account. I would never think of denying Jesus. Or would I?

My mind recalls a real-life experience when I, like Peter, didn't stand up for Christ. My parents had medical appointments one particular day and I wanted to meet them at the doctor's office to hear the report. As I drove there, I was tuned into Christian radio. The host of the show was talking about the previously mentioned passage. I wondered how Peter could do such a thing. He was with Jesus throughout his entire ministry and was a first-hand witness to his many miracles and teachings. I wondered if he had a sense of regret? A sense I would soon have.

As my parents consulted with the doctor, my mom handed her a business card from an internal medicine specialist who cared for my father when he was hospitalized several weeks earlier. The inside of the card read, "All healing comes from God. As a physician, I strive to provide the best possible care to help my patients in the healing process." When the doctor read aloud, "All healing comes from God," she said, "Hmph! That's interesting." Her tone was highly sarcastic as if *she* was the god who heals. There was a stirring in my belly and I wanted to tell her this was also my belief, but I said nothing. Absolutely nothing. And in my silence I denied Christ! I knew I should have spoken up, but it wasn't until the next morning during my daily prayer time that I was deeply convicted. I had just heard the message about denying Christ moments before walking in the doctor's office and now I was guilty of denying Christ through my silence! Praise God for His mercy, grace and forgiveness!

What are ways you might deny Christ in your daily life? Here are just a few examples I came up with. Can you relate to any of them?

- We fail to spend time reading God's written Word.
- Our faith walk doesn't match our "Christian talk."
- We don't spend time in prayer, communicating with, and listening to the Lord.
- We use inappropriate language, listen to inappropriate music, watch inappropriate shows, and tolerate inappropriate behavior, thus conforming to the ways of the world.
- We fail to give God glory when we do something good, highlighting ourselves instead.
- We try to control our own lives and destiny rather than placing it in God's hands, denying our trust in Him.
- We do and say things we would never do or say if we truly believed Christ was right by our side, in essence, denying His presence.
- We deny Christ in our silence, like I did.
- We ultimately deny Christ by not living by the standards He set for us in the Bible.

I wish I could have a do-over in the doctor's office again. I can only hope that this time I would have stood up for the One who laid down His life for me. Standing up for Christ doesn't mean you have to share the gospel, present the plan of salvation, or share your personal testimony. On that particular day, I could have simply said, "Yes, I also believe all healing comes from God."

CHALK TALK

Player Application

Deny defense is the act of a defender getting between the basketball and the person they are defending in an effort to prevent or discourage a pass to the person they are guarding. Is there anything getting between you and the Lord that would cause you from receiving the blessings He's longing to pass on to you? One of the biggest ways I believe we deny God is our time. Between school, homework, practice, work, and routine tasks, time is limited. But our time being limited doesn't mean we have to deny God. When we deny Him, we miss out on His power and blessings in our lives. This week, let your guard down!

Coach Application

Deny defense is all about great positioning—positioning that can shut down an offense, so in that sense it's good. However, in our daily lives, if we're not careful, we can put ourselves in a position where we're so busy and overwhelmed by life's demands that we end up shutting out God, ultimately denying Him our time and attention. Therefore, make a commitment to dedicate some amount of time every day to further develop your relationship with Him. Just as you have practice and game plans, find a devotional book or bible reading plan you can systematically follow. You can't deny that would be a wise investment of your time!

Parent application

We cannot reproduce what's not in us.

Parents, if we expect our children to openly talk about the Lord, we should set the example. In a recent sermon, my pastor said, "We cannot reproduce what's not in us." If we are ashamed to share what God is doing in our lives, then our children might be too. The Apostle Paul wrote in Romans 1:16, "For I am not ashamed of the gospel because it is the power of God that brings salvation to everyone who believes..." Begin in your home by having spiritual conversations every day. It's a great place to start!

PERSONAL TRAINING SESSION

- While Matthew 10:33 warns us about denying Christ, who does Luke 9:23 say we *should* deny? What does that mean?

_____

_____

- List three ways you may inadvertently deny Christ during the week. As you go about your week, how can you intentionally counteract these actions? For example, if you are not reading your bible during the week, make a declaration that you will read your bible three to five days this week for some amount of time.

_____

_____

_____

- Challenge yourself to memorize Matthew 10:33. Begin by writing it here.

_____

_____

POST-GAME PRAYER

Heavenly Father, open my eyes to see ways that I deny Your lordship in my life. The thought of denying You seems impossible, but I am willing to admit I subconsciously deny You through my silence, avoiding fellowship with You, and sometimes my behavior. I give You permission to lead my life today by yielding control to You. You've made it clear—if I want to follow You, I must deny myself and take up my cross daily (Luke 9:23). Just as the cross represents death, may I die to my selfish desires today and be more concerned with Your desires for my life, which are far better than I could even dare to dream. In Jesus' name I pray. Amen.

No Holding Back

There may be people that have more talent than you, but
there's no excuse for anyone to work harder than you do.
Derek Jeter

The difference between a successful person and
others is not a lack of strength, not a lack of
knowledge, but rather in a lack of will.
Vince Lombardi

You have only got three choices in life:
give up, give in, or give it all you've got!
Kim Garst

CHAPTER 15
NO HOLDING BACK

Do your best to present yourself to God as one approved,
a worker who does not need to be ashamed
and who correctly handles the truth.
2 Timothy, 2:15 (NIV)

HEADING INTO THE DISTRICT PLAYOFFS IN 2013, I posed a question to my middle school team: "What keeps you from being great?" I wanted each player to consider what was limiting them from being a more effective player. I got the typical answers. A few players said, "I lack confidence in myself." Others said, "I don't think I'm good enough." Some answers dealt specifically with skill, but one answer in particular peaked my interest. Transparent and guard down, one player answered, "I hold back." I was grateful for her honesty. "You hold back?" I asked. "Why would you hold back from giving God your best?" It sounded like a rhetorical question but I was searching for some real answers. The only answer she could give was, "I don't know."

Do you hold back from giving God your best? 2 Timothy 2:15a says, "Do your best to present yourself to God as one approved, a worker who does not need to be ashamed..." When you stroll out of the gym after practice, a game, or a tournament, can you honestly say you presented yourself to God as one approved? A worker who can truly be proud of your effort and not ashamed of your work ethic or attitude? What about in the classroom or at work? If you were to closely examine your efforts, would you be able to say you don't hold back from giving anything but your best? If you can easily answer "yes," then you might want to do some reevaluating. I'm not saying it's not possible to always give your best, but in over ten years of coaching, it's been rare that I've witnessed a player going *all out, all the time.* Why? Because it's hard!

God is not the kind of Father who desires half-hearted work.

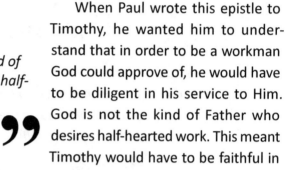

When Paul wrote this epistle to Timothy, he wanted him to understand that in order to be a workman God could approve of, he would have to be diligent in his service to Him. God is not the kind of Father who desires half-hearted work. This meant Timothy would have to be faithful in studying God's Word in order to handle it accurately and precisely. The King James Version reads, "Study to show thyself approved..." The Greek translation for "study" is to "be earnest or diligent." In other words, he was telling Timothy that in order to be approved as a workman for God, he was going to have to work persistently, rigorously, conscientiously, and with a sincere and intense conviction. Interestingly enough, the word for "approve" in this verse is translated "tested by trial." This tells us the labor of the workman is going to be tough. Therefore, Timothy was going to have to work diligently through the trials in order to present his best to God; approved as His workman, unashamed of his efforts.

What does this mean for you as a follower of Jesus and basketball player? It means the work you do, whether it's by yourself in the driveway or during a team practice, must be done diligently and earnestly, pushing through the trials that full-on effort brings—no holding back! It means you're flying around for every loose ball (not just the ones you think you can get), not hesitating on your defensive closeouts, communicating with your teammates (even when no one else on the floor is talking), attacking the rim with authority, running sprints with every ounce of energy you have left, and then running back to usher in that last player who is trailing the pack. It means you're showing up to practice like you're showing up for a job and leaving with a sense of accomplishment. And when that's all over, you will walk out of the gym drained of all your energy because you didn't hold back from giving your best effort...day in and day out. It takes an incredibly strong person, *physically and mentally*, to consistently play *and* practice this way. Not everyone will possess the passion necessary to be this type of player and that's okay. However, being aware of whether you're holding back or not could help push you to perform at a higher level.

I want to put you through an exercise right now. Wherever you're sitting, I want you to hold your right hand up as high as it will go. Yes, right now. I'll wait. Are you doing it? Don't put it down yet. Now, I want you to hold it even higher! Can you go a little higher? Well, what do you know! My guess is that you were able to hold your hand up just a smidge higher each time I asked you to. Did you hold back the first time? Perhaps you held back without even realizing it. Here's the point: You have no idea what your limitations are and how much more you are capable of until you actually give that extra ounce of effort you didn't realize you had in you. Think about that the next time you're competing in practice or a game. That extra ounce of energy just might make a world of difference!

CHALK TALK

Player Application

Try to remember the "extra ounce" principle when you're competing, no matter if it's in practice or in a game (and let's face it, you are competing with your own teammates in practice). Sometimes the slightest bit of extra effort on defense will help you get a fingertip on the ball, deflecting a pass just enough to be tipped into your teammates hands and resulting in a winning bucket. It does happen, but if you hold back, you'll never know what could have been. Have you been holding back in the realm of your spiritual life? How much effort are you putting into developing a stronger relationship with Jesus? It takes energy and time to work on your spiritual game too. Are you holding back in that area? If so, let's take the advice Paul gave Timothy by presenting ourselves to God as one approved; a worker who does not need to be ashamed and who correctly handles the truth. And in order to correctly handle the truth, we need to be in the Truth, which is God's Word. Challenge yourself to read the Bible or Christian material more this week than last week by using the "extra ounce" principle.

Coach Application

Do you have players who slack-off in practice and seem unwilling to unleash their full-potential? Sometimes players will give you their all, sometimes they won't. It's our responsibility to call out players who are holding back because of laziness, lack of desire, or lack of awareness. If we don't demand our players to practice at a level beyond what *they* think they can play at, we aren't doing them any favors. Paul held Timothy accountable by teaching him what he needed to do in order to be an "approved" workman and not ashamed of his efforts. Keep pushing your players to unlock their full athletic potential. And how do you rate as a coach? Do you hold back from giving your best efforts or are you fully invested in your players and the organization for which you coach? Set an example in your spirit, energy, and preparation.

Parent Application

What kind of a "worker" are you? If you're a stay-at-home parent, does your "workplace" resemble someone who works diligently and efficiently? If you work outside the home, are you an employee or boss who does just enough to get by or is there a greater purpose behind your work? Would God approve of the use of your time? Colossians 3:23 says, "Whatever you do, work at it with all your heart, as working for the Lord, not for human masters."

PERSONAL TRAINING SESSION

- Do a quick self-test. What kind of worker are you?
  a) I hold back and I'm aware of it.
  b) Sometimes I hold back and sometimes I don't.
  c) I rarely hold back.

- Read Revelation 3:15-16. Based on the answer you chose above, are you a "cold" player, a "hot" player, or a "lukewarm" player? What does God say about lukewarm works?

- Based on today's lesson, name one thing (tangible or intangible) you can demonstrate in your next practice or game to exhibit workmanship that will set you apart while presenting your best effort. Don't be afraid to think outside the box.

POST-GAME PRAYER

Gracious God, thank you for the wisdom that comes from Your Word. In Romans 12:2, You tell us not to conform to the pattern of this world but be transformed by the renewing of our minds. I confess that being lukewarm in my attitude and actions is so easy. Being a Christian and workman that is "hot" demands a different mindset—one that only the Holy Spirit can help me to achieve. I don't want to be satisfied with mediocrity. On the contrary, I want You to approve of my workmanship in *whatever* I do. Help me to engage with You daily so that I move further and further away from being a lukewarm Believer. In the name of Jesus Christ I pray. Amen.

The Consolation Prize

Satan was defeated by Christ at the cross, but he's
seeking you as a consolation prize.
John Piper

I know I have a place in heaven waiting for me because of Him,
and that's something no earthly prize or trophy could ever top.
Stephen Curry

My mother used to tell me man gives the award,
God gives the reward. I don't need another plaque.
Denzel Washington

CHAPTER 16

THE CONSOLATION PRIZE

When anxiety was great within me,
your consolation brought me joy.
Psalm 94:19 (NIV)

I WAS IN THE SEVENTH GRADE THE FIRST TIME I remember hearing the word "consolation." My basketball team was playing in a tournament and we lost one of our first games, so we were put on the "left-side" of the tournament bracket, the "consolation" side. Honestly, I had no idea what it meant. Years of basketball went by, and whenever my team played in the consolation bracket, I just figured it was a nice way of saying, "the losers' side."

Decades later, I had an "Aha!" moment while studying Psalm 94. I was sitting in a hotel room in College Station, Texas, awaiting my son's next tournament game. I paused at verse 19: "When anxiety was great within me, your consolation brought me joy." There was that word again—a word I had seen and heard many times since my youth, but this time the word "console" stuck out from the page. It made perfect sense now! I asked my son, "Hey, do you know what 'consolation' means in tournament play?" "Umm, not really," he said. "You're a loser? You're terrible?" I chuckled, remembering that's what I used to think, too. "I just learned something," I said. "What does it mean to console someone?" He answered, "To make them feel better." We both smiled as he had an "Aha!" moment of his own.

If you lose a game early on in a basketball tournament, you will likely find yourself on the consolation side of the bracket. It's not the side of the bracket any coach or team wants to be on, but if you happen to find yourself there, you could still walk away with a trophy. While it may not be the trophy you wanted to leave with, it does make you feel better. It does "console" you.

Ironically, as I write this devotional, my son's club team just experienced the very situation I'm writing about. They were playing in a "Great American Shootout" tournament and lost to two very dynamic teams on the first day of tournament play. Those two losses landed them in the silver bracket rather than the championship bracket. However, in the next three games, they played strong, dominating their opponents and winning the silver bracket. They went home with bag tags that read "Tournament Champions." No, they didn't win the overall tournament, but their victory in the silver bracket did bring some consolation.

Consolation isn't limited to the basketball court. The word "console" is defined as "comfort at a time of grief or disappointment." In Psalm 94:19, David expressed having great anxiety. But despite his anxiety, he received consolation from the Lord that brought him joy. A verse I often cling to is 1 Peter 5:7, "Cast all your anxiety on Him because He cares for you." God cares deeply when we are feeling anxious or downhearted. He wants us to look to Him for comfort and for consolation. No one, and I mean no one, can comfort us and bring consolation to our hearts like God can. In fact, in 2 Corinthians 1:3, God is called "the God of all comfort." Isn't that a beautiful thought?

My friend, you will most certainly find yourself in relationships and situations that disappoint you, but you have a permanent consolation trophy found in Jesus! He is your comfort! Don't look to anyone or anything to fill the gap that only Jesus can fill. Like David, you are going to have times when anxiety is gripping your heart. The New American Standard version of Psalm 94:19 puts it this way: "When my anxious thoughts *multiply* within me, your consolations delight my soul." If you are going through times of multiplying anxiety, stress, or depression, then allow Jesus to your console your heart! He lovingly invites you to run to Him with your weary heart and heavy burdens so He may give you rest (Matt. 11:28).

You will get knocked down. You will go through trials and tribulations in life. You will experience devastating losses, whether on the court or in life's daily battles. But make no mistake, in the lives of followers of Jesus Christ, there is no bracket other than the championship bracket. You have already won the victory when

But make no mistake, in the lives of followers of Jesus Christ, there is no bracket other than the championship bracket.

you accepted Jesus as your Lord and Savior. His sacrifice on the cross ensured that! "You see, every child of God overcomes the world, for our faith is the victorious power that triumphs over the world" (1 John 5:4, TPT). Without the cross, there is no hope. Without defeat, there is no glory. Without death, there is no life. But with the cross, there *is* hope. Despite defeat, there *is* glory. And because of Jesus's death on the cross, there *is* life. And that is a most wonderful consolation!

CHALK TALK

Player Application:

It's going to happen—you're going to lose battles. But friends, you have a choice. On the other side of our battles, we can continue to claw our way to victory (like my son's team did), or we can lay down in defeat. Our attitude will determine which route we choose. Will we choose to allow Christ to console us so we can rise up as joy-filled warriors, or will we allow the anxiety to eat us up? I know which route God would have us choose. Let's be victorious!

Coach & Parent Application:

After my daughter's team was eliminated in the semi-finals of the South Region Jr. NBA basketball tournament in the summer of 2018, her coach reminded them that the "L" didn't mean "loss" but "lesson." As a parent listening to the post-game speech, it brought me consolation. The team certainly learned some worthwhile lessons in that high-pressure event.

As with that Jr. NBA loss, most losses will have some measure of sting, but after the initial disappointment goes away, take time to look for some valuable takeaways that will bring some consolation. Remind your players that if they care to look hard enough, they will find some joy despite the defeat, and some good amongst the bad.

PERSONAL TRAINING

- According to Romans 5:3-4, what type of consolation (comfort in a time of disappointment) can come out of our trials and suffering?

_____

_____

- 1 Peter 5:7 directs us to cast our anxiety on God. Look up the definition of "cast," then explain in your own words what God is directing us to do with our anxiety.

_____

_____

POST-GAME PRAYER

Father, thank you for being the one who consoles. I confess that after a devastating loss, it's easy to focus on all the "should haves" rather than focusing on the things that might bring my heart consolation in time of defeat. Help me to fix my eyes on Jesus, the author and perfecter of my faith, to bring me out of the pit of despair, and to allow the Holy Spirit to replace my broken spirit with joy. Gently remind me of all the good lessons that can come from a loss when I look at things from Your perspective. In the power of Jesus' name I pray. Amen.

Waiting

Waiting is the hard work you must do so that God
can do the work that only He can do. Wait well.
Kay Harms

There is no greater harm than that of time wasted.
I've always believed that if you put in the work,
the results will come.
I don't do things half-heartedly because I know if I do
then I can expect half-hearted results.
Michael Jordan

The work that God does within us while we wait
is just as important as whatever it is we are waiting for.
Ben Patterson

CHAPTER 17

WORK WHILE YOU WAIT

Let us not become weary in doing good, for at the proper time,
we will reap a harvest if we do not give up.
Galatians 6:9 (NIV)

WHEN I WAS COACHING BASKETBALL AT THE REC-reational level, everyone got to play. The starting five would play the first five minutes, the next group of five would play the following five minutes, and they would rotate likewise for the second half. Playing time was not an issue. Parents were happy, players were happy, and I didn't have the pressure of trying to get everyone equal playing time.

For me, those days are long gone, and so are the days of equal playing time. Both of my teenagers are now playing on highly competitive teams against highly competitive opponents. The coach doesn't look down the bench with the same motives anymore. In tight games, not everyone will get equal playing time. In some instances, some players may not even get to touch the floor. I can tell you from experience, it's a horrible feeling for a coach, and we know it's a horrible feeling for the player. I would venture to say it's even worse for the parents.

When my son and daughter were in middle school, they were both named MVP of their respective basketball teams. They were the leading scorers and held dynamic roles. However, on their former AAU teams, they rarely started, and in some instances they sat the bench more than they played. Like any other parent, I wanted to see my kids get their fair share of playing time, but until they proved to their coaches that they deserved a starting role, or more minutes on the court, they were going to have to work while they waited.

Do you find yourself in this same position? Are you not getting the playing time you had hoped for? There could be a variety of reasons why. First and foremost, *maybe* you're not as skilled as some of the players on your team. If that's the case, keep working! Find extra opportunities to train outside of team practices or do some purposeful training on your own. Ask your coach what you need to work on to get better (and be ready for the answer). Go online and look up specific drills that will address those weaknesses. Don't just go out and shoot the ball. Anyone can do that. Practice with purpose. Set some objectives of what you would like to accomplish. Write those objectives on a note card and read it every day before working out! Evaluate yourself often and assess your progress. As you put in the work, push yourself to a place that feels uncomfortable. Work with great intensity until that work ethic becomes your normal, and then create a new normal.

Creating a new normal in your spiritual life would benefit your basketball goals as well. On the flip-side of your basketball goals note card, write down a couple of bible verses that inspire you to live out your daily life with the same passion as you're putting forth in basketball. I've learned that having a deep and personal relationship with Christ is indeed work, but it's the kind of work that yields the sweetest rewards!

Another reason you may not be getting the playing time you want is because you're not willing to work hard enough. Work ethic is more important than you might realize. Kevin Durant's favorite quote is, "Hard work beats talent when talent fails to work hard," [34] and I completely agree! Several years ago, I had to make cuts during tryouts. There was only one spot left on my middle school roster and there were two girls I was considering for that position. One of the players was more talented, but didn't show a great deal of effort. The other player was not as skilled but worked harder than the other. I ended up choosing the young lady who worked harder despite her lack of skill. It was a decision that shocked our small, private school community but a decision I stood by whole-heartedly. I believe a valuable lesson was taught and learned that season, a lesson I continue to share over and over.

When a coach sees you're willing to work harder than the rest of your teammates, you'll eventually catch his or her eye. Be consistent in your effort, not like a light switch—on one day and off the next. In the words of the legendary, Michael Jordan: "I practice as if I'm playing in a game so when the moment comes in a game, it's not new to me."[35] How do *you* practice?

Finally, how's your defense? You can be the best shooter in the gym, popping three-pointer after three-pointer, but if your defense is weak, you won't get the playing time you're hungering for. If the person you're defending can blow by you with a quick first step, that's a problem! Of course you're going to get beat from time to time, but if you're continually getting beat, you're going to find yourself on the bench. Everyone loves to practice with a ball in their hands, but how much time do you spend *(on your own)* becoming a better defender? Practicing footwork?

Footwork is a critical basketball skill that routinely gets neglected during practice time. It's a skill that needs to be developed on your own. If you would be willing to set aside ten minutes a day, three times a week or more, to specifically work on agility drills, you will find that your ability to stop, start, and change directions more quickly will improve at a rapid pace, allowing you to defend against your opponent more easily. Not only that, but offensively, good footwork will help you get to the rim more effectively as well.

Just as you must have good footwork to defend against your opponent, you have another adversary out there trying his best to trip you up—Satan. How can you counterattack his assaults against you? I would suggest the same way Jesus did—by submitting to the

Holy Spirit and arming yourself with Scripture! James 4:7 tells us that when we submit ourselves to God and resist the devil, he will flee from us! But in order to do this, we have to be willing to set aside time to learn how to submit to God and memorize scripture. Therefore, I will give you the same advice as I did about improving your footwork: Be willing to set aside ten minutes a day, three or more times a week to get better at it. The common theme here is WORK!

Those are just a few reasons why you may not be getting as many minutes as you'd like. If playing time is not an issue for you, then keep working hard to maintain your current position. In fact, push yourself to work even harder because you better believe someone is working to earn your spot. However, if you are not satisfied with your playing time, let me encourage you to keep working. Don't give up! The Apostle Paul said, "Let us not grow weary of doing good, for at the proper time we will reap a harvest if we do not give up" (Gal. 6:9 NIV).

Do you believe you are giving the best effort you possibly can but things still aren't working in your favor? God's word says, *at the proper time*, you will receive your reward *if* you do not give up! Player, do not lose heart! Keep working while you wait. The proper time is yet to come!

CHALK TALK

Player Application

I realize sitting the bench can crush your spirit. I was there myself during two tough years as a collegiate player. But one thing is for sure, I never gave up. It was in my DNA to work hard. If you are a child of God, you have devine DNA inside of you in the form of the Holy Spirit. Call upon the power of the Holy Spirit to help you put forth good work and a rigorous effort, never forgetting Colossians 3:23, "Whatever you do, work at it with all your heart, as working for the Lord, not for man." Lay aside your expectations of praise from your coach and work to honor the Lord instead. You are always enough for Him!

> " Lay aside your expectations of praise from your coach and work to honor the Lord instead. "

Coach Application

One day when I was challenged emotionally and mentally, the athletic secretary took a notecard off her bulletin board and handed it to me. It read: "Let us not become weary of doing good, for at the proper time we will reap a harvest if we do not give up." It had been a tough season! The team I was coaching was made up of incredible young women, but despite their unshakable determination they had a hard time pulling off the win. With the exception of two games, our losses were between one and five points the entire season. Talk about discouraging! So when I received the notecard that day, it was a turning point for me. I displayed it in my car where I could see it daily. It was a reminder that one day the harvest would come in if I didn't become weary or give up on my girls or myself. Well, the harvest did come in! The following season, we went undefeated in district play. We only lost two games that season by a grand total of three points. To this day, I still have that notecard.

Parent Application

If you son or daughter finds themselves in a similar situation, I would encourage you to remind them of Galatians 6:9 often. It can replace a crushed spirit with encouragement and hope. It's not just a great lesson for basketball, it's a great lesson for life. After we come to faith in Christ, we are told to combine our faith with good works. Doing good works (and not seeing any rewards) can become wearisome. But God sees your works and He will give you strength to keep going when you fix your eyes on Him. Be your child's number one cheerleader. Remind them how much you believe in them and that in the end, hard work pays big dividends.

PERSONAL TRAINING SESSION

- Read 2 Chronicles 15:7. What will happen if you stay strong and do not give up?

_____

- Read Colossians 3:23. Truthfully, who are you working for when you practice and play?

_____

- In regards to your personal life, what area(s) do you think you need to work on to strengthen your basketball skills? What can you do to strengthen your relationship with Christ?

_____

_____

_____

POST-GAME PRAYER

Father, You are sovereign and so is Your timing. Help me to be patient as I work while I wait. I confess that I rarely approach life or the game of basketball with the mindset of working for You and You alone. Thank you for the encouragement I receive from Galatians 6:9. Remind me that if I work, *as one working for You,* that I will reap a harvest if I do not give up. Help me not to become weary in doing good or working hard, but to call on the Holy Spirit to give me strength and perseverance, for Your power is made perfect in my weakness! In Jesus' powerful name I pray. Amen.

THE END

EPILOGUE

JUST DAYS AFTER SUBMITTING MY MANUSCRIPT for *No Other Gods,* the Lord began to strip things away from me one by one. Pluck. Pluck. Pluck. One of those things was basketball-related. For two days, I found myself weeping unexpectedly, feeling depressed, and I grieved relationships that I thought would be lost. It left me to ask the question: "Kari, are you sure *you* have not made basketball an idol?" Indeed, I believe I had.

For the next two months I found myself walking through uncharted territory, facing trials that I could have never predicted. I surrendered my will for God's will and relied solely on His loving hand of protection as He delicately took me through a refining process. Like the Israelites of old, I was taking a journey through the wilderness, hoping that the "Promised Land" would come sooner rather than later. I tried to map out shortcuts in my mind, yet I was fully aware that God's perfect plan for my life did not involve alternate routes.

What is God's purpose for us in the wilderness? In trials and tribulations? His purpose for me, you, the Israelites and for *all mankind* is the same: He wants our pure devotion. He wants us to desire Him above all else. He wants us to passionately pursue His heart. He wants us to worship Him and Him alone; to forsake all other gods or images in the form of *anything or anyone!* In addition, God wants us to experience His love while expressing our love for Him, even in the midst of our journeys.

The timing of the release of this book is no coincidence! Currently, in the face of COVID-19 (coronavirus), God is stripping humanity of a multitude of passions that take the place of Him.

Those passions not only include basketball, but a vast number of other sports as well. The NBA has suspended the season "until further notice" which has set in motion a tidal wave of reactions. The NCAA, NAIA, professional, high school, club, and travel teams have either cancelled or suspended their tournament seasons. Thousands of high school athletes that were scheduled to compete in huge college recruiting showcase events this summer will likely miss these opportunities. Sports families are beginning to feel empty. And that's exactly what I believe we are left to feel when our hearts are filled with anything but Him—empty; our hearts uninhabited of all the things that were potentially taking the place of God.

There is still so much that I don't understand about God and His ways, but I do know this: everything that happens is filtered through Him and that includes COVID-19. This global pandemic has many Christians reflecting on Second Chronicles 7:11-22, that urges people and nations to humble themselves, pray, and to seek the face of God; turning from our own ways and turning back to Him so that He can heal our land. In these Scriptures, God calls us to abandon false gods and bow down to Him instead of bowing down to the idols we have created, sports included. God places dreams and passions in our hearts that He wants us to pursue, but none of them are as important as the pursuit of Him.

Today, the very places where we gather to "worship" our favorite athletes and celebrities have closed their doors. Stadiums are locked, gyms are quiet, grandstands are empty, galleries are nonexistent, and even church buildings have had to shut their doors as recommended by medical experts at the national, state and local levels. However, for believers of Jesus Christ, we know that *the people* are the church and where the people are, the praises of the Lord will reign forever and the courts of the Lord are always open!

We have come to a crossroad: We can lay down our false gods and embrace the One True God, or we can search for new passions to pack back into our hearts. I don't know about you, but as for me and my house, we will serve the Lord.

March, 2020

BIBLIOGRAPHY

All About God. "Prayer of Forgiveness: Receive a New Life." Accessed February 28, 2020, https://www.allaboutgod.com/prayer-of-forgiveness.htm.

Bailey, Megan. "Christian Basketball Players Conquering the Game," Accessed February, 2020, https://www.beliefnet.com/entertainment/sports/christian-basketball-players-conquering-the-game.aspx.

Ball is Life. "About us." Accessed February 28, 2020. http://ballislife.com/about-us/.

Barnett, John Barnett. "The Sinners Prayer." Crosswalk, February 16, 2017, https://www.crosswalk.com/faith/prayer/the-sinners-prayer-4-examples.html.

Beyond the Ultimate. "Ruth Riley." Accessed February 28, 2020, http://www.beyondtheultimate.org/athlete/Ruth-Riley.

Bible Reasons. "Putting God First." January 7, 2020. https://biblereasons.com/putting-god-first/.

Bonham, Chad. "NBA All-Star Dwight Howard Talks About Family, Faith and Destiny." *Inspiring Athletes (Beliefnet)*. Accessed February 28, 2020, https://www.beliefnet.com/columnists/inspiringathletes/2011/12/nba-all-star-dwight-howard-talks-about-family-faith-and-destiny.html.

Budon, Jeremiah. "New Help Defense: Cavs Scream 'Help!' Whenever They're On Defense." *The Kicker,* June 4, 2017, note: website/url no longer available.

Dictionary.com. "Where does Ball Is Life Come From?" Accessed February 28, 2020. https://www.dictionary.com/e/slang/ball-is-life/.

DeVenzio, Dick. *Runnin' the Show: Basketball Leadership for Players and Coaches*. Austin, TX: Bridgeway Books, 2006.

DeVenzio, Dick. *Stuff Good Players Should Know*. Austin, TX: Bridgeway Books, 1983.

Durant, Kevin "My favorite quote is 'Hard work beats talent when talent fails to work hard.' Following that has helped me reach my goals #WinFromWithin," Twitter, January 4, 2012. https://twitter.com/kdtrey5/status/154694996233170945?lang=en.

Fine, Jerry and Marilyn Fine. *One on One with God Leader's Guide*. Enumclaw, WA: WinePress, 2003.

Goodreads. "Neal Maxwell Quotes." Accessed February 28, 2020, https://www.goodreads.com/quotes/45464-god-does-not-begin-by-asking-us-about-our-ability.

Hot Rock Nation. "AAU Basketball Fight Players Vs Refs." *YouTube*. July 8, 2018, https://www.youtube.com/watch?v=gV9WEQoXla8 (incident is at 5:03 in the video).

Kendrick, Alex. "White Chair Film—I am Second." *YouTube*. September 21, 2011, https://www.youtube.com/watch?v=XLcgf589P5U&t=33s.

Krueger, George and Mary-Lynn Foster. "A Challenge from Coach Wooden." *Big Success*. June 8, 2010, https://biggsuccess.com/2010/06/08/a-challenge-from-coach-john-wooden/.

Leccesi, Joe. "Five Most Common Questions About Verbal Commitments." *USA Today High School Sports*, April 27, 2017, https://usatodayhss.com/2017/five-most-common-questions-about-verbal-commitments.

Liew, Jonathan. "We say we do not like talking about referees but revel in using them as punching bags." *Telegraph*. April 16, 2016, https://www.telegraph.co.uk/football/2016/04/19/we-say-we-do-not-like-talking-about-referees-but-revel-in-using/.

Manrique, Bruno. "Stephen Curry on play against LeBron James: 'I was kind of like a chicken with his head cut off.'" *ClutchPoints*. June 5, 2017, https://clutchpoints.com/stephen-curry-against-lebron-james-chicken-head-cut/.

Merriam-Webster Dictionary. "Deny." Accessed April, 2018, https://www.merriam-webster.com/dictionary/deny.

Money, J. "Side Hustle Series: I'm a Referee (AKA I get paid to get yelled at)." *Budgets are $exy*. July 18, 2013, https://www.budgetsaresexy.com/side-hustle-series-get-paid-to-referee/.

NCAA. "Estimated Probability of Competing in College Athletics." Updated April 3, 2019, http://www.ncaa.org/about/resources/research/estimated-probability-competing-professional-athletics.

Officiating.com. "Referee Jokes."September 24, 2004, https://forum.officiating.com/general-off-topic/15536-referee-jokes.html.

Piper, John. "What is Idolatry." *Desiring God*, August 19, 2014, http://www.desiringgod.org/interviews/whit-is-idolary.

Prichard, Dr. Ray. "Is the Sinners Prayer Required for Salvation?" *Crosswalk*, July 11, 2012, https://www.crosswalk.com/blogs/

dr-ray-pritchard/is-the-sinners-prayer-required-for-salva-tion.html.

Ransomed Heart. "Prayer to Receive Jesus Christ as Savior." Accessed February 28, 2020, https://www.ransomedheart. com/prayer/prayer-receive-jesus-christ-savior.

Romano, Jason. "Stephen Curry Shares Christian Testimony at Liberty." *Sports Spectrum*, March 3, 2017, https:// sportsspectrum.com/sport/basketball/2017/03/03/ stephen-curry-shares-testimony-liberty/.

Spirituality & Health. "Jean-Paul Sartre on Commitment." Accessed February 28, 2020, https://spiritualityhealth.com/quotes/ commitment-act-not-word.

Sunday, Billy. "Billy Sunday Quotes," *Good Reads*. Accessed February 28, 2020, https://www.goodreads.com/quotes/27312-going-to-church-doesn-t-make-you-a-christian-any-more.

Taber, Duke. "Missing the Mark—The Definition of Sin." *Viral Believer*. Accessed February 28, 2020, https://www.viralbe-liever.com/definition-sin/.

TwoThreeForever. "Ahmad Rashad One On One Interview With Michael Jordan @ Age 50–2nd Three-Peat (1996-98)." Twitter, March 8, 2013, https://www.youtube.com/watch?v=r-WOC-SMC-Fc (see 3:51 mark in video).

WBIR Staff, "'God You're Good' | Tennessee Basketball Players Break for Baptism." *WBIR*, November 21, 2018, https://www. wbir.com/article/sports/college/vols/god-youre-good-tennes-see-basketball-players-break-for-baptism/51-616610823.

ENDNOTES

1 "About us," Ball is Life, accessed February 28, 2020, http://bal-lislife.com/about-us/.

2 "Where does Ball Is Life Come From?" Dictionary.com, accessed February 28, 2020, https://www.dictionary.com/e/slang/ball-is-life/.

3 John Piper, "What is Idolatry," Desiring God, August 19, 2014, http://www.desiringgod.org/interviews/whit-is-idolary.

4 "Putting God First," Bible Reasons, January 7, 2020, https://biblereasons.com/putting-god-first/.

5 Megan Bailey, "Christian Basketball Players Conquering the Game," Accessed February, 2020, https://www.beliefnet.com/entertainment/sports/christian-basketball-players-conquering-the-game.aspx.

6 Jason Romano, "Stephen Curry Shares Christian Testimony at Liberty," March 3, 2017, https://sportsspectrum.com/sport/basketball/2017/03/03/stephen-curry-shares-testimony-liberty/.

7 WBIR Staff, "'God You're Good' | Tennessee Basketball Players Break for Baptism," November 21, 2018, https://www.wbir.com/article/sports/college/vols/god-youre-good-tennessee-basketball-players-break-for-baptism/51-616610823.

8 Billy Sunday, "Billy Sunday Quotes," Good Reads, accessed February 28, 2020, https://www.goodreads.com/

126

quotes/27312-going-to-church-doesn-t-make-you-a-christian-any-more.

9   "Ruth Riley," Beyond the Ultimate, accessed February 28, 2020, http://www.beyondtheultimate.org/athlete/Ruth-Riley.

10 Duke Taber, "Missing the Mark—The Definition of Sin," Viral Believer, accessed February 28, 2020, https://www.viralbeliever.com/definition-sin/.

11 Chad Bonham, "NBA All-Star Dwight Howard Talks About Family, Faith and Destiny," Inspiring Athletes, accessed February 28, 2020, https://www.beliefnet.com/columnists/inspiringathletes/2011/12/nba-all-star-dwight-howard-talks-about-family-faith-and-destiny.html.

12 "Estimated Probability of Competing in College Athletics," NCAA, Updated April 3, 2019, http://www.ncaa.org/about/resources/research/estimated-probability-competing-professional-athletics.

13 George Krueger & Mary-Lynn Foster, "A Challenge from Coach Wooden," June 8, 2010, https://biggsuccess.com/2010/06/08/a-challenge-from-coach-john-wooden/.

14 "Prayer to Receive Jesus Christ as Savior," Ransomed Heart, accessed February 28, 2020, https://www.ransomedheart.com/prayer/prayer-receive-jesus-christ-savior.

15 Dr. Ray Prichard, "Is the Sinners Prayer Required for Salvation?" July 11, 2012, https://www.crosswalk.com/blogs/dr-ray-pritchard/is-the-sinners-prayer-required-for-salvation.html.

16 John Barnett, "The Sinners Prayer," Crosswalk.com, February 16, 2017, https://www.crosswalk.com/faith/prayer/the-sinners-prayer-4-examples.html.

17 "Prayer of Forgiveness: Receive a New Life," All About God, accessed February 28, 2020, https://www.allaboutgod.com/prayer-of-forgiveness.htm.

18 "Jean-Paul Sartre on Commitment," Spirituality & Health, accessed February 28, 2020, https://spiritualityhealth.com/quotes/commitment-act-not-word.

19 Joe Leccesi, "Five Most Common Questions About Verbal Commitments," USA Today High School Sports, April 27, 2017, https://usatodayhss.com/2017/five-most-common-questions-about-verbal-commitments.

20 Alex Kendrick, "White Chair Film—I am Second," September 21, 2011, https://www.youtube.com/watch?v=XLcgf589P5U&t=33s.

21 Jeremiah Budon, "New Help Defense: Cavs Scream 'Help!' Whenever They're On Defense," The Kicker, June 4, 2017, note: website/url no longer available.

22 Ibid

23 Dick DeVenzio, *Runnin' the Show: Basketball Leadership for Players and Coaches* (Austin, TX: Bridgeway Books, 2006), 50.

24 Dick DeVenzio, *Stuff Good Players Should Know* (Austin, TX: Bridgewood Books, 1983), 30.

25 Neal Maxwell Quotes, Goodreads, accessed February 28, 2020, https://www.goodreads.com/quotes/45464-god-does-not-begin-by-asking-us-about-our-ability.

26 Jonathan Liew, "We say we do not like talking about referees but revel in using them as punching bags," April 16, 2016, https://www.telegraph.co.uk/football/2016/04/19/we-say-we-do-not-like-talking-about-referees-but-revel-in-using/.

27 J. Money, "Side Hustle Series: I'm a Referee (AKA I get paid to get yelled at)," July 18, 2013, https://www.budgetsaresexy. com/side-hustle-series-get-paid-to-referee/.

28 "Referree Jokes," Officiating.com, September 24, 2004, https://forum.officiating.com/general-off-topic/15536-refer-ee-jokes.html.

29 "AAU Basketball Fight Players Vs Refs," Hot Rock Nation, July 8, 2018, https://www.youtube.com/watch?v=gV9WEQoXla8 (incident is at 5:03 in the video).

30 Bruno Manrique, "Stephen Curry on play against LeBron James: 'I was kind of like a chicken with his head cut off,'" ClutchPoints, June 5, 2017, https://clutchpoints.com/stephen-curry-against-lebron-james-chicken-head-cut/.

31 Jerry and Marilyn Fine, *One on One with God Leader's Guide* (Enumclaw, WA: WinePress, 2003), 119.

32 "Deny," Merriam-Webster Dictionary, Accessed April, 2018, https://www.merriam-webster.com/dictionary/deny.

33 Ibid

34 Kevin Durant (@kdTrey5), "My favorite quote is 'Hard work beats talent when talent fails to work hard.' Following that has helped me reach my goals #WinFromWithin," Twitter, January 4, 2012, https://twitter.com/kdtrey5/status/15469499623317 0945?lang=en.

35 TwoThreeForever, "Ahmad Rashad One On One Interview With Michael Jordan @ Age 50–2nd Three-Peat (1996-98)," Twitter, March 8, 2013, https://www.youtube.com/watch?v=r-WOC-SMC-Fc (see 3:51 mark in video).

ABOUT THE AUTHOR

KARI KIEPER IS BOTH A coach and discipleship facilitator. Those two passions have created a pathway for Kari to share Jesus Christ within her church and community, and while coaching and interacting with club teams and parents.

Kari gave up several scholarship offers to begin a career as a hairdresser during her senior year of high school, but her love of basketball drew her back to the game a little over a year later. Kari traded in her shears for a backpack and a ball when she accepted an offer to play at the University of Mary Hardin-Baylor in Belton, Texas. During her four years at UMHB, Kari received multiple awards for her tenacious defense and hustle. During her sophomore year, she broke a university record for the most free throws made in a single game. Kari's senior year was highlighted when she married her husband of almost thirty years, the evening before a conference game.

Kari finds her greatest joy in coaching at the grassroots level; when kids are most impressionable in forming their character and are ripe for learning solid, basketball fundamentals.

Kari resides in Leander, Texas with her husband and two teenagers.

CPSIA information can be obtained
at www.ICGtesting.com
Printed in the USA
FSHW020500130520
70193FS